LEADERSHIP UNIVERSITY

RYAN C. GREENE

LEADERSHIP UNIVERSITY
2nd Edition
52 Weekly Leadership Lesson On Becoming The Leader Others Will Beg To Follow

Cover design by: GreeneHouse Media, Print Division
Photography courtesy www.istockphoto.com

ISBN: 978-0-9842631-9-6
Printed in the USA

Published by
GreeneHouse Media
www.greenehousemedia.com

great-sounding studio and show how you can make a huge difference in your room for as little as $150.

Audio Mixing Boot Camp: Hands-on Basic Training for Musicians (Alfred Music)
If you're creating your first mix and don't know where to begin, or your mixes aren't as good as you'd like them to be, this book is here to help. It features a series of hands-on mixing exercises designed to show you how to listen and work like a pro, and reveals the tips, tricks, and secrets to all the different facets of mixing, including instrument and vocal balance, panning, compression, EQ, reverb, delay, and making your mix as interesting as possible.

Audio Recording Basic Training: Hands-on Survival Manual for Musicians (Alfred Music)
A beginners' guide to producing great recordings. The book features a series of hands-on recording exercises designed to show you how to listen and work like a recording pro, and reveals the tips, tricks and secrets to all the different facets of recording, including miking a drum kit, recording vocals, and miking electric and acoustic instruments.

Abbey Road To Ziggy Stardust (with Ken Scott) (Alfred Music)
The memoir of legendary producer/engineer Ken Scott, who holds a unique place in music history as one of only five engineers to have recorded the Beatles and was producer and/or engineer on six David Bowie records (among his many other credits). In this funny, poignant, and honest account, Ken pulls no punches, telling it as he saw it.

BOBBY OWSINSKI LYNDA.COM VIDEO COURSES

Audio Mixing Boot Camp. Almost nine hours of movies outlining the various steps, tips, and tricks of mixing like the pros.

Audio Recording Techniques. A five-and-a-half-hour course that describes how to record crisp, rich vocals and instrument tracks and covers the process of miking and tracking a complete song using A-list session musicians in a top-of-the-line studio.

Mastering for iTunes. A short video that demonstrates best practices for mastering music and audio destined for sale on Apple iTunes with its new Mastered for iTunes high-resolution audio program.

Audio Mastering Techniques. A two-hour video that explores essential mastering concepts and techniques used by experienced audio engineers to create a cohesive album from a set of mixed tracks.

Also Available From Bobby Owsinski

Delay Genie iPhone App: Time your delays and reverbs to the track with this free, easy-to-use app that also has a live mode for delaying speakers or delay towers.

Bobby Owsinski's Social Media Connections

Bobby's Music Production Blog: bobbyowsinski.blogspot.com

Bobby's Music Industry Blog: music3point0.blogspot.com

Bobby on Facebook: facebook.com/bobby.owsinski

Bobby on YouTube: youtube.com/polymedia

Bobby on LinkedIn: linkedin.com/in/bobbyo

Bobby on Twitter: @bobbyowsinski

About Bobby Owsinski

A long-time music industry veteran, Bobby Owsinski started his career as a guitar and keyboard player, songwriter, and arranger, eventually becoming an in-demand producer/engineer working not only with a variety of recording artists, but on commercials, television, and motion pictures as well. He was one of the first to delve into surround sound music mixing, and has worked on more than 100 surround projects and DVD productions for a variety of superstar acts.

By combining his music and reording experience with an accessible writing style, Bobby has become one of the best-selling authors in the music recording industry. His 18 books are staples in audio recording, music, and music business programs in colleges around the world.

Bobby is a frequent speaker at universities and industry conferences the world over, he has served as the longtime producer of the annual Surround Music Awards, and he is one of the creators and executive producers for the Guitar Universe and *Desert Island Music* television programs.

Bobby's blogs are some of the most influential and widely read in the music business. Visit Bobby's production blog at bobbyowsinski.blogspot.com, his Music 3.0 music industry blog at music3point0.blogspot.com, his postings at Forbes at forbes.com/sites/bobbyowsinski/, and his website at bobbyowsinski.com.

DEDICATION

This book is dedicated to the leader you are about to become.

ACKNOWLEDGEMENTS

As usual, first, I want to acknowledge my Lord and Savior, Jesus Christ. Thank you for using me as your vessel to spread your principles and teachings to the business community (even if they do make me sneak it in sometimes). Every time I quit on my purpose, You were there to bring me back.

My wife Tyneka- God knew what He was doing when he put us together. You have been my everything since Day One. Thank you for taking this journey with me. My (now adult) children, Jordan and Jayden- Watching you two grow up has been the joy of my life. You two are already such great leaders. I have loved every minute of watching you to chart your path and walk in your gifts.

I want to acknowledge all the voices that go unheard and unrecognized simply because you are too young, too old, too black, too white, too urban, too corporate, too rich, too poor, too under-educated, too over-educated, too elitist, too Joe The Plumber, too Wall Street, too Main Street, too big business, too small business, too feminine, too masculine, too gifted, too challenged, too religious, too secular, too conservative, too liberal, too straight, too gay, to hip-hop, too country, too assertive, too lazy or too anything else. You don't need anyone else to validate your beliefs or your significance. Don't get caught up chasing titles and approval from people but always focus on chasing purpose and approval from God!

Finally, I want to acknowledge every person who has ever had a dream too big for anyone else to understand. Always know that nothing is too hard for God and if He said it then it is so! Dream on, Dreamer! Don't lose yourself with trying to be "The Next Someone Else" but focus on becoming "The First YOU" and you will find success beyond your belief. Let this book help you move from being a Dreamer to a Doer!

Course Syllabus

Welcome Address: The World Still Needs Your Leadership

Senior Year

Capstone Course

Final Exam

WELCOME ADDRESS

THE WORLD STILL NEEDS YOUR LEADERSHIP

Since 2001, I have taught leadership all across the globe. My primary focus has always been on teaching people how to first lead themselves so they can be equipped to lead others. Becoming a better leader has nothing to do with getting a promotion on your job. It has nothing to do with getting a new title. It has nothing to do with your boss, family, co-workers, or subordinates. The first person you must learn to lead is yourself and this book is the perfect tool to assist you with that daunting task.

Now before you close the book and go off saying "*I'm already a great leader*" or "*I know all there is to know about leadership*", let me first say I beg to differ. Secondly, even the best leaders are lifelong learners who not only continue to work on their own growth, but they then help others around them become better leaders too.

No one has all the answers and no one teacher is going to reach every student. My hope is that this book taps into parts of you like no other self-help book has before. My goal for this book is to systematically assist you over the course of the next 52 weeks with your own personal leadership development through the weekly lessons, activities and reflections.

1

This book, like all my previous books, is going to require some effort on your part. I want you to not only read the information, but to honestly work through the activities and questions so that you can grow into a better leader and live the life you were designed to live. This is the first time I've put my entire collection of leadership lessons from my other books into one resource such as this.

Over the next 52 weeks you will be fully equipped to take the role as the leader in your life and apply what you learn to your personal, business, and professional life. I don't want you to make the mistake of reading this book all the way through like you would read a novel. This book is designed to be read one chapter per week so that you have time to actually implement what you learn and grow weekly in your leadership development. Every week you will be taught a new lesson on leadership and given a new area upon which to focus. Be sure to make note of your takeaways, journal your thoughts, and push yourself to grow as a leader.

The bottom line when it comes to leadership is that it has nothing to do with your title and everything to do with your influence. When you speak do people listen? When you move do people follow? When you call do people answer? You must become the leader you want to be before your business card says you are.

Let me start right out by saying, this book is not for every student. This book is only for those students who are ready to look life in the face and claim their success as leaders. This book is for those students who know they've been designed for something bigger in their life- something bigger than mediocrity. This book is designed for those students striving to reach higher levels of success regardless of their current position in life. This book is for those who are looking to walk in the office of leader and not just wear the title.

If you are any one of the people I described, then welcome to the book that will set you on the course to amazing success. It is your time to master your personal leadership and walk in your destiny and purpose. You will get out of this book everything you allow yourself to get out of it. If you are a willing student, I am your willing teacher. Welcome to Leadership University. Class is in session!

LEAD 101:
DEVELOP A STRONG WHY

Having success is great but you must develop a reason why you want success. That's what this chapter is about. This first key to unlocking your success as a leader is perhaps the most important and vital key. That key is having a strong Why. Knowing why you strive toward any goal is more crucial than the goal itself. A Why is your driving force. It makes you get out of bed early on a rainy morning to work toward your goal. It keeps you up late at night when you're exhausted and feel like you cannot do anymore. It is what makes you do the impossible and achieve the unbelievable. Just like a soldier on a war mission, your Why is your mission statement for your existence so don't take it lightly.

Too often people start a mission with a goal in mind when in actuality to maximize your success potential you need to start with why you even want the goal accomplished. Be careful not to confuse your Why with your goals. Your goal may be to be a millionaire but why you want to be a millionaire will determine whether you ever become one (even before you ever take the first step toward it). Take a minute to think about your Why. Why are you willing to go through whatever it takes to achieve your goals? Why can't you stop pursuing your dream even after you've failed time and time again? <u>Your Why is your engine that gives you power to go; your goal is the end destination you seek, and your strategy is the roadmap you take to get there.</u> Everything else, the books, seminars, associations etc, will be what tunes you up to get to where you are going as quickly as possible.

Getting to the end is what we all seek but without an engine we're in for a long trip. This chapter is not intended to tell you your Why. I can't do that. You must determine that for yourself. What I can help you with is how to determine your Why for yourself. My life changed for the better once I figured out exactly why I existed and why I was pursuing my dreams, consequently, I am assured that once you develop a strong enough Why you will be well on your way up the ladder to success.

There are four questions that you should explore and answer to develop your Why.

1. WHAT MOTIVATES YOU?

Is it your family? Is it your career? Do you like helping other people? Do you like to be recognized for what you do? Do you want to be rich? Do you need more time in your life? Do you like to travel? Do you have kids? Do you want kids? Are you married? Do you have a ministry within you? Do you like to play instruments? Do you sing or dance or write? What do you do well that you can't do as much as you'd like to because of your current life situation?

These questions should be enough to get the juices boiling in the right direction. Answer these questions honestly and use the answers as your starting point toward your Why. If you are going to spend any part of your life pursuing anything worthwhile then you must want to do it and you must enjoy the journey. Finding out what motivates you will help to keep you pushing through the storm even when you have no umbrella.

An overwhelming majority of workers in America are dissatisfied with their current jobs. They feel exploited, underappreciated, and disenfranchised; however, they continue to sacrifice their time, their life, and their dreams for something they passionately hate. They are not motivated to go above and beyond at work because the return is too often not worth the sacrifice to get it. However, the more motivated and fulfilled you are by something the more you are willing to go through to achieve it. When developing your Why, take serious consideration about what motivates you to action. A Why is not worth the paper it's written on if it's not going to push you toward achieving your goals.

2. Who Or What Is At The Center Of Your Why?

Most unsuccessful people find themselves constantly struggling to reach higher levels in life because their reason why only revolves around themselves. Everything they do begins with the question, "What's in it for me?" They want success because they want to buy things or gain recognition or even appear above others. On the contrary, most successful people have Whys that are centered on someone or some cause other than themselves. Their blessings come because of a desire to make an impact on someone else's life. They've learned to place the needs of others before their own.

Think about it, we have a much easier time letting ourselves down than letting others down. We let ourselves down all the time and just keep on going on with life. How many times have you said, "I'm going to lose weight", "I'm going to go back to school and get a degree" or even "I'm going to start my own business" but you never did it. It was easy to let yourself down. What if you would have said, "I'm going to lose weight so I can live a long life and be around for my family", "I'm going back to school in order to have more to offer to those that count on me" or "I'm starting my own business so that my grandchildren will never have to work and run from bill collectors". Notice the difference? When you do things for others it becomes more difficult to quit when things get rough.

You don't want your great grandchildren to see your picture in the family photo album 50 years from now and ask, "Who is this" and their parents say, "That's your great granddad. He really let us down. He always said he was going to start a business, but he always said tomorrow. He always said he would sacrifice today so that we would not have to work but he listened to his negative friends and gave up on his dreams. Here's your great grandmother, she always quit when things got rough and let her fear take over instead of fighting through her troubles. She always said God would provide all her needs and she could do all things through Him, but I guess she never really believed it."

That's a sad situation but the reality is that it happens every day. When your Why is centered on the right people or purpose it will drive you harder and push you through the pain more than if it were just about you.

3. Is It Strong Enough To Make You Cry?

Your Why can't be weak. "I want to be rich" is not strong enough. Ninety-seven percent of people will never be rich so to want to be rich is more than likely not motivation enough to keep you going through the hard times you will face trying to become rich. You need to evaluate the reason why you want to be rich and focus on that. Your Why must be so strong that if you quit before you're done it will make you cry. My mentor and friend Michael Humes told me this some time ago and I had to revamp my whole reasoning. This is why, as I stated earlier, most successful people's Why is not even about them. It is almost always centered on making life better for someone else.

How much longer are you going to settle for being average simply because it's easier than working hard to achieve excellence? How long are you going to be afraid to answer your phone because you know it's a bill collector? How long will you wonder whether your car will still be outside each morning? How long will you prostitute your skills and abilities to a job you hate just to get a check instead of building something for yourself? How long are you going to live outside of God's will for your life yet expect Him to fix everything for you?

Take an honest inventory of your current life situation and ask yourself if you like what you see. How do you feel about where you are in life? Have you reached the levels of success you thought you would by this time? The sad reality is most people are not happy. Instead of getting depressed about where you currently are, use that to push you toward where you can be. When you realize there is a way out and you don't want to be where you are then quitting will never be an option. If the thought of you quitting does not bring tears to your eyes because of how it is going to affect you and those depending on you, then your Why is not strong enough.

4. IS IT WORTH DYING FOR?

Dr. Martin Luther King Jr. said, "If a man has not found something worth dying for, then he is not fit to live". His Why was to have equality for all races and it was, to him, a Why that was worth dying. Think about all the opposition that Dr. King fought against to achieve his Why: the hatred, the police arrests and brutality, the house and church bombings, the constant stress on he and his family and ultimately his life. All for people that he did not even know. So, what's stopping you? Are your obstacles really that big? Had Dr. Kings Why only been about him, his name probably would have never been mentioned in the history books because he would have quit long before the first news story could have ever been written. But even at the age of 26 he understood the power of having a cause worth dying for and it motivated him to change the way an entire country was governed. It is because of the Why he possessed almost 50 years ago that I can even write this book today and anyone who desires to read it can read it. Don't take your Why lightly; someone else 50 years from now will be counting on you to make his or her life better.

Asking yourself is something worth dying for does not mean you are asking death to knock on your door or that you are literally going to die because of it; however, it does state that death is the only thing that will stop you from pursuing your

Why. That's a huge advantage over others that don't have that. When your back is against the wall and there seems like there's no way out, as long as you're alive you can keep on fighting. That cannot be taught. Having a strong enough why will give you that attitude automatically.

Paul of the Bible said he died daily to sin so he could live for Christ. What is it that you need to die to so that your life will be better? <u>Why wouldn't you be willing to die for financial freedom when you are already killing yourself simply to live check to check?</u> Instead of spending your time complaining about your life, find someone whom you would go through anything for to make his or her life better. Being willing to die for your Why gives you the resolve to say, "<u>I will...Until</u>" and never give up.

If you haven't done so already take a few minutes now to go through these four questions and develop your Why and WRITE IT DOWN. Use it as your starting point to unlocking the best leader within yourself. Once you realize why you want to be a successful leader it becomes easier to figure out how to become one.

Chapter Takeaways:

_____

_____

_____

_____

_____

_____

_____

_____

_____

_____

_____

_____

How Will I Implement This Lesson?

_____

_____

_____

_____

_____

_____

_____

_____

_____

_____

_____

LEAD 102:
YOU MUST GROW YOUR MINDSET BEFORE YOU GROW YOUR PAYCHECK

One of the most flagrant means by which leaders cheat themselves is by not feeding their mind through consistent personal development. A USA Today poll showed that 25% of Americans polled have not read a single book in the last year. I have heard numbers even higher than that. Regardless of your age, all that you know today is not enough to get you through the rest of your life. Even if your mission in life is to simply skate through and do nothing with your life, every day you must learn new ways to survive by being the best worthless bump on a log you can be. I define Personal Development as "increasing your value in the marketplace." When it comes to personal development I live by the mantra "You must become the person you want to be BEFORE your business card says you are."

If you aspire to be a great leader, then you must follow the best practices of great leaders. You must read the books they read, get the coaching they get, do the things they do. You must become that person in your mind and in your practices before you actually become that person in your position. What good would come out of you being elevated to a position that you were not mentally equipped to fulfill? God will not put more on you than you can bear so if you are not mentally ready to bear the responsibilities that go with higher levels of leadership then you will not be elevated to those positions.

Life is not fair, life is just. Life gives you what you earn and not simply what you want. You may *want* to be the Sales Manager at your job but if you do not study your craft, learn to work with others, develop your leadership skills, put in the extra work, and grow into that position; then you have *earned* the right to be just an account executive. You may *want* to earn $250K a year but as long as you demand your company gives you a set salary as opposed to you earning unlimited bonuses, complain about how much life sucks, focus on the problems and not the solutions and get paid for what you do instead of what you know; then you have *earned* your $50K a year lot in life. If you want more, you must grow more.

In my first book *Success Is In Your Hand* I introduce the "Personal Development Puzzle." For an in-depth look at how you can begin making personal development a natural part of your everyday life I would encourage you to purchase that book and work through the exercises. For now, I will share some of the bullet points on the Four Keys to the personal development puzzle.

Key #1: Watch what goes into you. The basic tenet of personal development is taking care that you fill your mind with positive inputs. To get good things out you must first put good things into you. Reading self-help books like this one shows you are serious about filling your mind with positive life changing messages.

Key #2: Watch what comes out of you. When you begin to change what goes in you it inevitably changes what comes out of you. Everything from your attitude, your vision, your appearance, to the way you treat other people will begin to improve. People will begin seeing a difference in you probably before you even see the difference. You will begin to attract other like-minded people who will play major roles in your success.

Key #3: The Law of Associations. As you begin to grow on the inside, your senses will be more alert to the destructive behaviors and people with whom you were once connected. Your current friends will either have to change their mindsets and grow with you or you will ultimately outgrow them. A tell-tale sign that you are on the right path with your growth will be when your friends get angry with you and tell you that "you changed."

Key #4: Appreciate who you become along the way. Personal development is a lifelong journey. There is no finish line or final destination where you can say "I've arrived." The joy is in the journey and knowing that you have become a better person along the way. Unlocking your full potential and walking in your designed purpose is the ultimate reward for a life dedicated to personal development.

Chapter Takeaways:

_____

_____

_____

_____

_____

_____

_____

_____

_____

_____

_____

_____

How Will I Implement This Lesson?

_____

_____

_____

_____

_____

FRESHMAN YEAR

_____

_____

_____

_____

_____

_____

_____

LEAD 103:
You Must Have A Big Vision

In John C. Maxwell's book *21 Irrefutable Laws of Leadership,* he discusses the "Law of Navigation." The Law of Navigation states that anyone can steer the ship, but it takes a leader to chart the course. Navigators see the whole trip before the ship even leaves the dock. They see more than others see, they see farther than others see, and they see before others see. While there may be many people on the ship, it is the leader who gives the direction in which the ship will sail. The crew may have many ideas and thoughts but there is only one captain and only one course.

The Law of Navigation can be summed up in one small but powerful word- VISION. Vision is probably the single most critical element of leadership. It is the leader's vision upon which all other principles are built. It does not matter how charismatic you are, how influential you are, how qualified you are or even how many times you read this book and others like it. People follow leaders because they have a vision that is much bigger than their own and they feel that the chosen leader has the aptitude to bring the vision to fruition.

People will only follow leaders once they buy into their vision. If you are having a difficult time getting people to fall in line and buy into your leadership then perhaps it is because they have not yet bought into your vision. Give yourself a vision check. Do you see a brighter tomorrow or are you stuck in yesterday's problems? Do you dream that the impossible is in fact possible or do you limit your efforts to only the realm of what is realistic?

Successful leaders are successful because they focus on the solutions and not the problems. They focus on the destination and not the twists and turns in the road. Having a big vision enables you to see the final results before the methods of achieving those results have even been conceived. If you stay focused and help others see the promised land through your eyes and get them to attach themselves to your vision, you will be amazed at how much more of an effective leader you will become.

Vision, however, can sometimes get those who have it in trouble because they can see things as if it were right in front of them while others without that vision just cannot. Vision caused Joseph to be sold by his own brothers into slavery, vision caused John the Baptist to be beheaded, and vision even caused Martin

Luther King Jr., to be assassinated. What are you willing to go through to fulfill your vision? People are looking for a cause to fight for, a crusade to embark upon, and a vision to grab hold of and make their own. If your vision is big enough it will draw more than enough people to make you a tremendous leader.

Chapter Takeaways:

_____

_____

_____

_____

_____

_____

_____

_____

_____

_____

_____

How Will I Implement This Lesson?

_____

_____

_____

_____

_____

_____

_____

_____

_____

_____

_____

_____

LEAD 104:
YOU MUST HAVE A BURNING DESIRE

Burning: *Increasing fury*

Desire: *Conscious impulse toward an object or experience that promises enjoyment or satisfaction in its attainment*

Successful leaders have a burning desire to do their best. When you look at the definitions of the two words it really brings it into perspective. Great leaders must have an increasing fury toward attaining success because of the satisfaction its attainment will bring. Successful leaders have the attitude that there is nothing that will quench that desire but the fulfillment of their dreams or goals. As you develop your leadership and search for your purpose, an easy way to determine if you are heading in the right direction is by measuring your desire to do it. God is not going to call you to do something you are not driven to do. Even if you try to run from your called purpose, the desire still remains.

I have a burning desire to impact and change the lives of others in a positive way. That burning desire pushes me to write more books, speak to more people, do more radio shows, teach more seminars, train more people, and build more businesses. Even when my physical energy is low and depleted, it is that burning desire that keeps me going. What do you have a burning desire to achieve? What is it that makes you say, "I'll do it, or I'll die"? That's the thing right there. That is the key to your success. Focus your energy and resources toward that thing which you have a burning desire for and watch how things begin to change in your life. Watch how success will begin to chase you down. People will flock from everywhere seeking to be led by you.

It is hard for ambitious people to understand why other people do not have ambition. No one can teach you to be driven and ambitious. It is something that you either have or you don't, you are, or you aren't. Ambitious people were not taught to be ambitious, so they find it difficult to understand why everyone does not just want more out of life and why more people are not willing to do whatever it takes to get there. I would take a less talented athlete with a strong will to win over a more talented athlete with little desire. You can teach anyone the skills to be successful at anything, but you cannot force anyone to want to be successful.

If there is something that you want but you are not able to motivate yourself to move toward it, then maybe your desire for that thing is not strong enough. Perhaps you need to reevaluate your desires and be honest with yourself as to what you really want. When you have a burning desire for something, you cannot just sit idly doing nothing to move yourself closer to fulfilling your desire.

Chapter Takeaways:

_____

_____

_____

_____

_____

_____

_____

_____

_____

_____

_____

_____

How Will I Implement This Lesson?

_____

_____

_____

_____

_____

_____

_____

_____

_____

_____

_____

_____

LEAD 105:
STAY AWAY FROM NEGATIVE PEOPLE

Who is your dream killer? In 1993 Willie Jolley told my freshman class at Hampton University to stay away from dream busters. I cannot tell you another thing he said but that one thing has stuck with me all these years and I hope it sticks with you. How often have you bounced an idea off someone and they said it would not work or that you could not do it? Or how about those people who can never find a positive thing to say about anything?

Negative people will find everything wrong with an idea and focus on why it will not work instead of finding the positives and helping you ensure that it will work. The reality is that most negative people cannot see *themselves* succeeding so they displace that negative attitude on others and disguise it with sayings like "I don't mean any harm but..." or "I don't want to see you get hurt."

Negative people are like plagues, even worse they are like mental parasites slowly eating away at your positive mindset and destroying all your success cells in order to make you into another loser like them. The only fortunate thing about the disease of negative people is that there is a cure. STAY AWAY FROM THEM! Too many people destroy their lives and accept failure all because they are worried about what others will think. Too many dreams are lost forever because would-be successful leaders abort their dreams prematurely due to complications brought on by friends and family.

Why would a married couple struggling in their relationship only go to single people for marriage counseling? Why would a Christian go to a Buddhist to ask about salvation? Why would a success driven person who wants more out of life go to a negative, dream stealing, bad attitude having, complaining and complacent underachiever for advice on how to get ahead just because that person is your husband, your mother, or your best friend? If you want to become a successful leader and would like to free your mind of the negative influences attacking it, then you must be firm in your resolve to stop listening to negative people. If someone does not have what you want, and they are not actively trying to get it, then their opinion does not matter.

You are responsible for what signals you allow to filter into your brain. It is hard enough to lead effectively with a clear and positive mind so why would you make your job any more difficult by having to sort through the mess of countless negative inputs? The Law of Attraction states that we attract what we subconsciously focus on in our minds. Therefore, if you allow negative people to fill your mind with doubt and fears of impending failure then all you will attract to your life is doubt and failure.

Most of the time negative people disguise themselves as our friends and with friends like that, who needs enemies? If a crazy psychopath were chasing you with a knife and screaming they're going to kill you, you would either run for your life or stay and fight for your life. The negative people in your life are just like those crazy psychopaths only they are chasing your dreams trying to kill them. The crazy thing is that most of the time we just sit and watch them slice our dreams to shreds with their words and do nothing to stop them. Don't you think it is time you stand up and either run from those negative people or fight for your life? Your dreams are depending on you to fight for them.

Chapter Takeaways:

_____

_____

_____

_____

_____

_____

_____

_____

_____

_____

_____

_____

How Will I Implement This Lesson?

_____

_____

_____

_____

_____

_____

_____

_____

_____

_____

_____

_____

LEAD 106:
COMMIT TO THE PROCESS

Becoming a successful leader is a process. There is a divine order in which events must occur for you to reach your place of destiny. Along the way you will encounter obstacles and roadblocks that you must overcome. You will have people come and go in and out of your life. You will have days when you feel like you are on top of the world and other days when you feel like the whole world is on your shoulders. There will be some tough decisions you will have to make and certainly some sacrifices along the way. Success does not come easy, but it does come to those who stay true to the process.

Successful leaders are like oysters that have a tiny piece of sand caught in their shell. The oyster lives on the ocean floor surrounded by sand yet it can keep the sand from entering its shell. However, every now and then a piece of sand gets lodged inside the oyster's shell. That sand causes the oyster severe irritation and discomfort. The oyster must fight through the pain of the sand in its shell and find a way to overcome that difficult period. The oyster uses it own power within to fight the sand by covering it in calcium and proteins until finally a pearl is formed. The oyster has gone through a tough period in its life, but it transformed a negative situation into a precious jewel.

In leadership, trouble surrounds us on all sides just like the sand does the oyster. Hard times will come but it is up to us to make pearls out of every situation. Each person's process may be different but yours is the exact process that you need to go through. I never claimed achieving success in leadership would be easy, if that were the case there would be no need for books on the subject, however, knowing that if you just stick things out then success is inevitable enables you to appreciate the process and learn from it. Knowing there is a process you must go through and staying committed to it by not trying to shortcut your way to success will keep you focused and ultimately lead you to victory.

Walking in your destiny does not mean your life will be free of obstacles but it does make it easier to face the obstacles life brings your way when you know you have been called to do what you are doing. I remember hearing God clearly speaking to me and saying, "You are chosen." It was amid a very difficult time in my life and His confirmation that He had chosen me gave me all the motivation I needed to press on. All the ups and downs, the loneliness, the obstacles and such, are just part of the process of making you into what He purposed you to be.

What would happen if you mixed flour, baking soda, raw eggs, sugar, butter, vegetable oil and water in a bowl and ate it? You would probably get very sick and at the very least have to fight to keep it down. What if you took that same concoction and instead of eating it you put it in the oven on 350° for 40 minutes? Now you have a wonderful, yummy cake. What's the difference? The process. Life is just like baking a cake in that you will have all kinds of ingredients coming together to make you. Some will be good like sugar and others will be not so good like raw eggs but when you put them all together and add a little heat to it, everything turns out great.

Everyone's process is going to be different but rest assured, everyone has a process. Have you ever heard, "If you can't stand the heat get out of the kitchen?" The intensity of the heat you can endure is an indicator of your growth through the process. A cake must be baked at 350° because it cannot handle 400°. The same is for you. God will not give you more than you can bear so stand firm and don't run from your process. Think about the importance of the process you go through. Your trials and tribulations are the heat that molds and shapes you into a successful person. Some trials may not even be directly for you but never lose sight of the importance of your process. There is something God is trying to get out of you and only the fire can

LEAD 106: #THEPROCESS

purge it. ~~Success does not come by just going through the process~~ but from *growing* through the process.

Chapter Takeaways:

_____

_____

_____

_____

_____

_____

_____

_____

_____

_____

_____

How Will I Implement This Lesson?

_____

_____

_____

_____

_____

_____

_____

FRESHMAN YEAR

_____

_____

_____

_____

_____

LEAD 107:
SET A STANDARD OF EXCELLENCE IN ALL YOU DO

Undoubtedly at some time we have all found ourselves uttering the words "That's so ghetto" about something or someone. Perhaps some company's young receptionist was unprofessional with you or maybe during opening prayer the deaconess at your church asked the Lord to forgive the First Lady for wearing that same black hat every Sunday. Whatever your experience may have been, we have all been there at one time or another asking, "What in the world were they thinking?" We laugh at the folly of others and chalk it up as ghetto; however, you are in serious trouble if you are the one being called ghetto.

If you want to attract more people and build a reputable brand, then you must live by a higher standard. You must set a standard of excellence in all you do. If you want to compete with, and hopefully one day become, the best then you must act, think, look, and operate like the best today. You may not have written the most books, but you can certainly make sure that your books are excellently produced. You may not have the biggest sales department, but you can strive to make sure your salespeople provide excellent service to your clients. Excellence cannot be measured quantitatively or by how much you have but it is measured qualitatively or by how well you use what you have.

When you set a standard of excellence in your organization, it lets those working with you know that you only expect the best. It also sends a sign to those whom you serve that you will only give them your best. Whether it is putting 100% effort into every project, starting every meeting on time, or wearing a suit to work on dress-down day; every detail plays a significant role in how you and your leadership is viewed by others. When you pursue excellence, those around you will also begin to pursue that same high mark. The more excellent your leadership becomes the more excellent your results will be.

When people understand that you expect excellence from them it will prevent them from coming to you with just any kind of mess. They will begin to try to solve the simple problems themselves instead of bombarding you with problems they should be able to fix on their own. The more they grow the bigger the problems they will tackle. They will take pride in their performance and begin to imitate your excellent behavior. If you want to see your people grow and become better leaders, then start by setting a standard of excellence that promotes independent thinking and problem solving.

Chapter Takeaways:

_____

_____

_____

_____

_____

_____

_____

_____

_____

_____

How Will I Implement This Lesson?

_____

_____

_____

_____

_____

_____

_____

_____

_____

_____

_____

LEAD 108:
THERE ARE NO SHORTCUTS TO LONG-LASTING SUCCESS

Today we live in a microwave society where everyone wants everything quick, fast and in a hurry. We want money NOW, we want big houses and fancy cars NOW, we want a spouse and 2.5 children NOW, we want to be famous NOW and we want to be the boss NOW. The longer we must wait for things to happen, the more impatient we become, the more we try to force things to happen. The more we see those around us progress the more ground we feel we are losing on them. The more we see The Jones achieve the less we feel there is left for us to achieve. But I believe that certain things like pot roast, apple pie and success just taste better when they're slowly cooked in a conventional oven.

Some things you just cannot rush, and the sweet taste of success is one of those things. Surely no one enjoys dealing with the pain of failures, the loss of friends, or the economic, physical, and emotional hardships that one may have to endure while striving to reach their full potential and grow as a leader; however, if you want an apple pie you must cut the apples, prepare the crust, and then let it bake. It is the baking process that takes the longest and is the most painful, but it is through that very process that all the ingredients bind together to form the wonderful, finished product.

If you think about it, a human's journey is not much different than that of an apple. What if when the apple was growing on the tree, instead of just learning how to be a good apple and waiting until it was fully prepared to fulfill its assignment, it got impatient, thought it knew all it needed to know about being a successful apple and jumped off the branch to go out on its own. Although the apple may still be good for some things, it will never grow to its full ripeness (potential). Only the apples that have weathered their growth process will ever make it to a grocer's stand.

Even then, the baker looks at the apple and realizes that even though it is pretty and shiny on the outside; only what is on the inside really matters. The baker then begins to peel away the skin of the apple. The very façade the apple has spent its whole life perfecting is now being ripped away. Everything that once hid the impurities and imperfections is taken away and the true nature of the apple is revealed for the world to see. Next, the baker takes the big bad apple and chops it into manageable pieces. The apple learns that bigger is not always better and that you can serve more people if you are willing to share yourself with others.

The baker then realizes that the apple itself is not good enough for a pie, so he begins to surround the apple with other ingredients. Where the apple cannot carry the weight of being a pie alone; a little butter softens the apple, some sugar and cinnamon sweetens the apple, and a thick flaky crust protects the apple from the heat. Once the group has been assembled, it is time to put them in the oven under intense 350° heat for 50-60 minutes. If the apple can survive the heat of the baking process it will come out more valuable than it was when it began. The apple would have achieved greater success and helped more people along the way.

As leaders, when we try to find shortcuts for success and jump off the branch too early it often leads to mediocre unfulfilled lifestyles. Even if you luck up from time to time, you may never become a pie. What if you were designed to stay rooted and become an apple tree? We are all just a single apple. Those who try to rush success serve a handful of people and are gone forever. Those who patiently live out their destiny and weather the growing pains go on to become apple trees, share their fruit with thousands of people every season and live forever. Do not cheat yourself by trying to rush long lasting success.

Chapter Takeaways:

_____

_____

_____

_____

_____

_____

_____

_____

_____

_____

_____

How Will I Implement This Lesson?

_____

_____

_____

_____

_____

_____

FRESHMAN YEAR

_____

_____

_____

_____

_____

LEAD 109:
YOU MUST HAVE HIGH INTEGRITY AND GOOD CHARACTER

No one likes a cheater. Whether it be relationships, sports, business, or anything else; no one likes a cheater. The sports world was turned upside down in the early 2000's due to multiple steroid scandals and accusations of cheating in baseball and track and field. The business world is constantly turned upside down by accounting scandals and financial fraud by more companies than I can list. It seems as if people have thrown integrity and character to the wind in exchange for temporal gains. When it comes to whether you are a "good" person or not, actions definitely speak louder than words.

One of the easiest things to lose and yet the hardest thing to get back is your good name. Successful leaders learn this early on and understand how important character and integrity are to achieving success. In life, it does not matter how trustworthy you think you are or what a caring person you believe yourself to be. What matters is how others perceive you in those areas. What others perceive to be true about you is their reality about you regardless of how true or false their perception may be. It is critical that the perception you think you are giving off matches the perception you're actually giving. It didn't matter how many times athletes like Barry Bonds or Roger Clemens insisted they never used steroids, the perception of many was that they and others used them so that has become the reality for them in the minds of those people even 20+ years later.

Good character can be summed up as the positive qualities you possess. How do you treat people? Are you trustworthy? Are you easy to be around? What morals and values govern your life and shape your character? Remember, factors as small as just being on time can have a major impact on your character in the eyes of others. You do not want to be known for always showing up late for everything. Some people may see you as irresponsible or untrustworthy. Once someone labels you it is almost impossible to erase that label. Learning to be more conscious of things you say and do and thinking more about how your actions affect others will help you to develop a favorable character among others.

High integrity is your uncompromising adherence to a code of moral values. Having values and standing by them speaks volumes about a person. Successful leaders do not lie, steal and cheat to get ahead. Having integrity means you do the right thing even when no one else is around. It means your word is your bond. If you say you are going to do something, then you get it done. People want to work with people they can trust and the more people who trust you, the larger your network of available resources grows. The larger your network of resources grows; the larger your success as a leader grows.

It seems as if it's getting harder and harder to find leaders that not only cherish integrity and character from others but are walking the walk themselves. It is easy to point out the flaws in others, but you must be willing to live up to the same high standards you set for everyone else. We are living in a world today where it is more and more difficult to find people you can trust. An easy way to stand out as a leader would be to simply maintain high integrity and good character. If people cannot trust you, they will not follow you.

Chapter Takeaways:

_____

_____

_____

_____

_____

_____

_____

_____

_____

_____

_____

How Will I Implement This Lesson?

_____

_____

_____

_____

_____

_____

_____

_____

_____

_____

_____

LEAD 110:
GREAT LEADERSHIP ATTRACTS GREAT PEOPLE

In 2006, the book and film, *The Secret* took the literary world by storm. Everyone was clamoring to find out what was the great secret to abundance and success. Millions of people were searching for this great secret to getting everything they ever wanted out of life and being more successful than they ever dreamed. If people were not buying the DVD they were buying the book. Oprah Winfrey and other talk show hosts did several shows spotlighting the authors and contributors of the book. I, along with millions of other people, went online or to the local book retailers to purchase and read this great secret only to find out that the "secret" was no real secret at all.

All of the hoopla and publicity that ultimately lead to hundreds of millions of dollars being made all revolved around one principle called *The Law Of Attraction*. This secret that you attract into your life the things you think about in your mind is nothing new. *The Secret* simply took a Biblical principle and cleverly repackaged it, commercialized it and marketed it to the masses, but they left out one key element. *The Secret* would have readers believe that the power to create your own abundant life lies solely in each of us simply by the thoughts we think and the results we attract. This packaging removes the need for God giving us the power to orchestrate our own lives (a dangerous thought considering what some of us would do with that power if we had it).

God tells us in Psalm 37:4 to "Delight yourself in the Lord and He will give you the desires of your heart." In Hebrews 11:1 we are told that "Faith is the substance of things hoped for, the evidence of things not seen." God tells us in Matthew 6:33 to "Seek first the kingdom of God, and His righteousness; and all things will be added unto you." Proverbs 16:3 says to "Commit your works unto the Lord, and your thoughts shall be established." Even in Proverbs 18:21 we are warned that "Death and life are in the power of the tongue." God has been telling us since the beginning of time that our thoughts attract our reality but the real secret, if you want to call it that, is that God creates the reality - not us. True abundance and success only come when we put Him first in our thoughts and actions.

What greater leader has ever walked the Earth than Jesus Christ? His message and vision was one that attracted great people who were willing to forsake all else to follow Him. Christ's followers believed so strongly in where He was leading them that they were willing to ultimately sacrifice their own lives to spread His message. Over 2000 years after the birth of Christ, His message is still attracting people to follow Him today. A message that started with one man and spread to twelve has now spread to millions and before the end of days His message will spread to every person on the planet. Now that is great leadership!

Laurie Beth Jones authored the best-selling book *Jesus CEO* in which she uses the wisdom of Jesus to teach readers how to lead like Christ would lead. She uses the reasoning that if Christ was able to reach the entire world, then if we use Him as our example of a great leader, we surely can attract more than enough great people to succeed at anything we do. None of us will ever be as great as The Greatest but the greater the leader we become the greater the people we will attract. And that's no secret at all!

Chapter Takeaways:

_____

_____

_____

_____

_____

_____

LEAD 110: #GREATLEADERSHIPATTRACTS

_____

_____

_____

_____

_____

_____

How Will I Implement This Lesson?

_____

_____

_____

_____

_____

_____

_____

_____

_____

_____

_____

_____

LEAD 111:
DON'T PROCRASTINATE

Brian Tracy wrote a book on overcoming procrastination entitled "Eat That Frog." It was a best-selling advice book that promised to teach you everything you ever wanted to know about breaking free from procrastination and was written by one of the world's greatest Sales Trainers. He used the example of eating a frog as a metaphor for that daunting task in front of each of us that we continually put off.

I borrowed the book from the library twice but kept putting it off and never read the book. Go figure. Finally, I got the book on CD and listened to it in my car, and I have been eating frogs ever since. Time waits for no man and one of the biggest enemies to successful leadership is procrastination. You could have done all the research, met with all the right people, weighed all your options to come up with the perfect plan of action; however, if you do it too late, it is like you never did it at all.

One of my biggest pet peeves is to hear people justify their procrastination, poor planning, and laziness by saying "I work better at the last minute." How would you know you work better at the last minute if you have never gotten a project done ahead of schedule to compare the two outcomes? Of course, you *feel* like you work better at the last minute. You have no choice but to get the work done. It is the last minute. Most procrastinators are not used to working hard but cramming a 3-month project into 3 days is hard work. Therefore, procrastinators feel that since they worked hard it must be good work. I would venture to say that overwhelmingly that is not the case.

What would happen if a boxer decided that instead of training the traditional 6 weeks leading up to a fight that he (or she) would only train for 12 hours a day the last three days leading up to the fight? He would probably go into the fight saying something like "I worked really hard. I'm in the best shape of my life. We got a lot of work done in a short period of time." Then after the fight he would probably say something like, "I don't know what happened. I thought I was prepared. Did anyone get the tag number on that truck that hit me?" As a boxer it would be ludicrous to wait until the last minute to prepare for the biggest fight of your life and think you could jump in the ring and compete. So why would you do it in your life and profession? You may not be jumping in the ring against Mike Tyson but as a leader you are constantly fighting and sparring against the competition. Why would you tie one hand behind your back by procrastinating? In leadership you must always have "The eye of the tiger" and be prepared to pounce on every opportunity.

I want to give a challenge to all my procrastinators. On your next major project, set a schedule to complete your project one week earlier than the due date. This will allow you to work more efficiently, do proper research, test your results, make any changes and upgrades, relieve unnecessary stress, and keep you from locking yourself in your office for three days wearing the same smelly sweat suit with cold pizza and a case of Red Bull ™. Once you accomplish that, evaluate your results and how it made you feel to pace yourself through a project and really give it your best. I am willing to bet it will only take once for you to change your thinking and strive to "Eat that frog" every time.

Chapter Takeaways:

_____

_____

_____

_____

_____

_____

_____

_____

_____

_____

_____

_____

How Will I Implement This Lesson?

_____

_____

_____

_____

_____

_____

_____

_____

_____

_____

_____

LEAD 112:
ENJOY THE JOURNEY

One thing I hate is driving on long road trips. I have about a four-hour limit behind the wheel and after that I am ready to jump out of the car. I don't know how truck drivers do it driving for 10-12 hours at a time. But even as much as I hate driving for long periods, there is one thing I hate even more. I cannot stand it when my passengers, my so called "road dawgs", on my trip fall asleep in the car while I'm driving. What the heck did I bring you for if I have to listen to your snoring for 6 straight hours? How alert do you think I will be if, with the wind in my face from all four windows down, I have to still fight to hear the blaring radio over the deafening noise of your grizzly bear like snoring?

It is always the very ones who are begging to go on every road trip that fall asleep before you even use the first quarter tank of gas. I literally almost died driving to Atlanta when my singing group was trying to get a record deal because everyone in the car fell asleep including me. All I remember was driving through South Carolina while it was dark and the next thing I remember, I was awakened by the noise strips on the shoulder of I-85. The sun was up and looked like it had been for quite a while. We were about two feet from the median wall and that close to meeting our Maker. A car full of guys and nobody had my back and stayed up with me. They all wanted to get to Atlanta and get a record deal, but no one wanted to endure the journey of the 10-hour drive.

The average person's life is much like one long 76-year road trip. We all have a destination at which we are seeking to arrive. Each of us will Google the best way to get there before we leave. Some of us may choose the fastest way while others may choose to avoid the highways and take the back roads. Some may choose to travel by plane, train, or bus. Some will rent someone else's car, and some may drive their own vehicle. Some will travel by the light of day and others will travel under the darkness of night. Regardless of the choices we make to get there, our focus is usually on our destination.

The problem arises when we get so focused on trying to get to our destination that we fail to enjoy the journey of getting there. If you always fly so that you can arrive in a hurry, then you may never experience the hidden treasures found in slowing down and taking those slow winding country roads. If you always jump into someone else's vehicle because it is safer and less risky than driving your own, then you will never experience the joys and pains of using your own vehicle to successfully arrive at your destination. If everything you do, you do in the dark, then you will never experience the fullness of walking in the light.

Everyone's journey is unique to that individual. We have all been equipped with the necessary AAA coverage plan to get us through any flat tires and breakdowns we may experience. The important thing is to always stay moving towards your destination and to take time out to enjoy the journey. Learn to enjoy each phase of your growth and the lessons that come with each level of promotion. Do not get caught up trying to rush destiny or thinking you can arrive early. The doors will only open at the appointed time. We were given peripheral vision for a reason. While we should keep our eyes focused on the road to our destination, our peripheral vision still allows us to enjoy the sites along the way.

Chapter Takeaways:

_____

_____

_____

_____

_____
_____
_____
_____
_____
_____
_____
_____

How Will I Implement This Lesson?

_____
_____
_____
_____
_____
_____
_____
_____
_____
_____
_____

LEAD 113:
TODAY'S ACTIONS DETERMINE YOUR FUTURE LIFESTYLE

I once heard it said that where you are today is a direct result of the decisions you made 5 years ago. That means if you are unhappy with your current situation in life then all you must do is look back five years ago and look at the choices you made and that will answer all your questions as to why you are where you are today.

If you are financially unhappy then probably five years ago you made some poor financial decisions that put you in an uncomfortable financial situation now. If you are dissatisfied with your personal relationships, then five years ago there were some decisions you made that adversely affected your ability to be in a happy relationship today. But the past is the past and no matter how much we would love to we cannot go back and change the past. Therefore, we must make better decisions now to secure our desired lifestyle in the future.

I used to coach high school football in Baltimore County and one of the things that really disturbed me about the young guys was that so many of them had no clue just how great an impact their choices in the moment would the rest of their lives. I don't know when it became cool for kids to be dumb and uneducated, but it wasn't always like that.

The street lifestyle is celebrated in every form of media and our kids have fallen for the trap. Everyone wants to get paid from basketball or rap, but no one is talking about going to college or starting your own business. Our youth seem more interested in earning a rap sheet than earning a college degree. The thing I tried to get through to them was that one day they were going to look back and wish they would have taken advantage of the opportunities they had the first time.

I see so many people fight to overcome regrets of missed opportunities and trying to get back the time they let slip by. Normally it is around age 25-30 when most people look up and ask "What am I doing? Where did the time go?" They begin to realize that they are all grown up and it is time to start taking life seriously and planning for the future. The good thing about life is that as long as you are alive it is never too late to start living. If there is one thing I wish I could drill into the minds of everyone I meet it would be to "Make the most of every day."

Too many people are making short term investments in activities that will yield fleeting returns while losing focus on the long-term goals for their life. You must start acting today if you want to be successful in your future. You must start acting today if you want to be a millionaire in your future. You must start acting today if you want to be a philanthropist in the future. You must start acting today if you want to live a lifestyle of abundance and fulfillment in the future.

Chapter Takeaways:

_____

_____

_____

_____

_____

_____

_____

_____

_____

_____

_____

LEAD 113: #TODAYSETSUPTOMORROW

How Will I Implement This Lesson?

_____

_____

_____

_____

_____

_____

_____

_____

_____

_____

_____

_____

_____

LEAD 201:
MAKE A DECISION

This may seem simple and elementary, but it is amazing how many people struggle with simply making a decision. You may come up with great ideas, but eventually you must make a decision as to which ideas you are going to pursue. Leaders are faced with decisions every day. As a leader, people are counting on you to make decisions they either cannot make themselves or do not want to shoulder the responsibility of making. Some decisions are easy to make, while others are tough enough to really challenge your heart and backbone as a leader. Great leaders is able to quickly and diligently weigh all the options and come up with a decision that is best for the vision and purpose of the organization or group he or she leads.

Effective leaders understand that every decision is not going to make everyone happy. Organizations, groups, teams and even families should have clear missions and goals in mind. It is up to the chosen or appointed leaders to make the proper decisions that will accomplish those set goals. Have you ever worked under a leader who when asked to make a decision always asked, "What do y'all think?" or said, "It's up to you."? Or one of my favorite replies from weak leadership when forced to decide is, "Why don't we take a vote?" People elect leaders to be the face of a group of people and to carry out their best interests. Leaders should gather information through effective communication with those whom they lead so that they are aware of the wants and desires of their people; however, when it's time to decide, the great leaders do not struggle with making the tough decisions because they always have their people's best interest at heart.

I want to stress the importance of "effective communication with those whom you lead." Some leaders have the misconception that as leaders they do what they want, and the people will just have to follow them and pay the price for their ill-informed decisions. Elected politicians are guilty of this crime of poor leadership. Making tough decisions is not what makes you a great leader. Quality leaders understand that their job is to serve those whom they lead by developing a vision and mission that can be eagerly adhered to because it is based on proper information gathering and by evaluating the hearts and opinions of the people they serve.

If you lose sight of your people's needs, eventually your people will see that they do not need you and you will be replaced. Corporate CEOs, Athletic Coaches and Religious Leaders are usually given a much shorter leash, as compared to Politicians, when it comes to making proper decisions as it relates to the organizations they run. For some reason people seem more willing to look the other way and ignore their politician's lies and lack of effective decision making. Does anyone remember "Mission Accomplished"?

No one wants to follow a leader with no backbone, nor does anyone want to follow a leader who thinks they know it all. As a leader you must not only make decisions for yourself, but for those who call you leader.

Chapter Takeaways:

_____

_____

_____

_____

_____

_____

_____

_____

_____

_____

_____

_____

How Will I Implement This Lesson?

_____

_____

_____

_____

_____

_____

_____

_____

_____

_____

_____

LEAD 202:
PLAN YOUR EXIT STRATEGY BEFORE YOU EVEN BEGIN

I am surprised by how many business leaders and entrepreneurs I meet that have no exit strategy for their business. They just work their business day and night and have never thought about how they plan to ever get out. Many business owners think they are supposed to work their business until either they or their business dies- which ever happens first. I was taught a long time ago that the purpose of starting a business from scratch is to build it into a profitable business and then sell it to someone else.

I know it may sound crazy but think about it. Do most people start their own businesses to work for the rest of their lives or do they start businesses to make money for the rest of their lives? For most people the answer is the latter. Why not get the money up front and let someone else run the business while you move on to bigger and better things?

Wouldn't it be much better if someone gave you $100 Million today for your business as opposed to you having to work 70 hours a week for 20 years to earn $100 Million in your business? Look at what happened with the dot com business era. Many people started businesses and sold them for billions of dollars like Mark Cuban. He then went on to buy an NBA Basketball Team, The Dallas Mavericks.

Others went public and sold their companies to shareholders like eBay® and Google®. Unfortunately, there were many other dot com business owners who did not have a well thought out exit strategy and stayed in too long and lost everything. Look at companies like Facebook® and YouTube® who within a few years of starting their businesses were both sold for over $1 Billion each. Why would you not sell your company for that kind of money?

Whenever you start a business, get involved with an organization or take on any new project, you should have an exit strategy already in place. You should already plan your departure before you even walk in the door. You cannot get so emotionally attached to your business or your position that you lose focus of your long-term goals. The best thing about business is that you can always start another one. Take my media company for instance; even though I love GreeneHouse Media, and I love the work we produce, I have an exit strategy in place and a dollar amount that will get me to sign over the majority control of my company (don't give up the whole thing). Once I am no longer the majority owner you know what I can do? I can take that money and go and start another company the next day!

Now when do you think I came up with that master plan? It was before I even wrote my first book *Success Is In Your Hand* in 2005. The same thing can be true for you. Don't let your love for what you do stop you from making a generation changing payday because you don't want to sell your business. Contrary to popular belief, it is possible to do what you love to do and be rich at the same time. Plan your exit strategy, sell your business and if you really love what you do then start another company minus the financial stress of trying to make ends meet. As a leader you must be able to visualize the end before you even begin.

Chapter Takeaways:

_____

_____

_____

_____

_____

_____

_____

_____

_____

_____

_____

How Will I Implement This Lesson?

_____

_____

_____

_____

_____

_____

_____

_____

_____

_____

_____

LEAD 203:
Don't Spread Yourself Too Thin

Growing up as a kid I used to hate pound cake. My mother used to make them all the time and sprinkle it with powdered sugar. I hated it because it was so dry, but most of all because it did not have any frosting on it. I have always had a sweet tooth so having a cake without frosting just did not make much sense to me. I used to call it the "grown up" cake. I think the only thing worse than a cake with no frosting is having a cake with not enough frosting. At least a pound cake is not supposed to have frosting, so you know going in what to expect. But nothing turns my taste buds more than going to a party and seeing a sheet cake with some thin, skimpy layer of just enough frosting. Like I am not supposed to know there was supposed to be more frosting, but you only bought one can. Frosting was not designed to be spread too thinly and neither are great leaders.

Has anyone ever told you that you are not Superman? Are you guilty of trying to do way more than you can physically or mentally handle? If you answered "Yes", then you are probably guilty of spreading yourself too thin. No matter how much you desire to be, you cannot be involved in every group or every activity that comes along. Sometimes as a leader you must learn to say the most powerful two-letter word in the English language "NO." You must be strong enough and value your time enough to be able to tell people when you simply cannot take on any more work.

It is not a leader's job to run around pulling their hair out trying to be in every place at once. You cannot serve on every board or be in every meeting. You cannot lead every choir or run every aspect of practice. There is an important leadership concept that the sooner you learn it and apply it to your leadership the sooner you will become a better leader. That concept is: Delegation. The best leaders learn how to spread the tasks among other up and coming leaders on their staff. The worst thing you can do as a leader is fall into the trap of thinking you have to do everything yourself to get it done right. If that is the case in your situation then that still falls on your leadership shoulders since you are the one who selected your staff of incompetent people.

By avoiding the temptation to spread yourself too thin, this frees you up to actively do one of the leader's most important jobs- think. As the leader you are the visionary of the team and if you never have a free moment to think and plan a course of action then your team will have no direction. Your team depends on you to come up with bright fresh ideas and to keep them motivated. If your brain is constantly overloaded from all the mundane tasks you have to do, then you will lose motivation and it will be impossible for you to motivate others. Everyone loves a great party, but what's a great party without a cake? If you want to motivate your team, start by bringing them a cake and make sure it has extra frosting that's never spread too thin.

Chapter Takeaways:

_____

_____

_____

_____

_____

_____

_____

_____

_____

_____

_____

How Will I Implement This Lesson?

_____

_____

_____

_____

_____

_____

_____

_____

_____

_____

_____

_____

LEAD 204:
KEEP THE MAIN THING THE MAIN THING

One trap that I have had to learn to overcome is the trap of losing focus on the main thing. When you are building several companies, and you want to see them all grow it is easy to sometimes lose focus and try to do everything at once. Even though my companies worked together for one common purpose, it became impossible to build them all effectively at the same time. Each year I found myself asking, "Who am I going to be this year in my business and what will be the main hat I wear for the upcoming year?" One year I focused on being a motivational speaker, another year I focused on being a talk show host, another year it was something else.

As an entrepreneur it's easy to fall into the trap of trying to do everything, but it's hardly ever effective in building a thriving enterprise. Pareto's 80/20 Rule states that 80% of any project gets done by 20% of the people. In business this translates to 80% of your revenue will be generated by 20% of your products or services. Knowing this fact, now you can see why it is so important to keep the main thing the main thing.

If 80% of your success comes from 20% of your people than it should be clear that although they only make up a small number of your staff, you better treat them with care and nurture that 20%. The problem is that the 80% that only generate 20% of the results often time try to demand 100% of your time and energy. I see leaders far too often get sucked into spending all their time with 80 percenters thinking that by spending time with them they can help them be more productive. In theory this sounds like it makes sense, but in practice, the most successful leaders spend the most time fostering and nurturing the 20 percenters because clearly that is where their bread and butter lies.

Look at any sales organization and you will see that 80% of the sales are generated by the top 20% of the sales force. At any restaurant 20% of the menu items generate 80% of the revenues. The other 80% simply make the menu look nice. It is critical to your success to keep the main thing the main thing and to not be swayed by "the next big thing" every time it rolls around. Someone will always have the next big business venture or the next big internet idea or the next big wave in whatever, but you must stand firm, know what makes you who you are and keep focused on the main thing. If you want to experiment, then experiment with the 80%, but leave the main thing alone. Find ways to nurture it, build upon it and make it better but always keep the main thing the main thing.

Chapter Takeaways:

_____

_____

_____

_____

_____

_____

_____

_____

_____

_____

_____

How Will I Implement This Lesson?

_____

_____

_____

_____

LEAD 205:
SCHEDULE SOME TIME OFF

Here is where the well-planned spontaneity comes in. I know it is an oxymoron but so is jumbo shrimp and they are still the first thing to go at every party. I understand how busy the life we lead can be. We work 8-10 hours a day, then the kids have soccer, dance, and karate practice. Then there is church and bible study, organizational meetings, walking the dog, working out at the gym, studying for school, asking people to join our million-dollar home-based business, washing the dishes, still staying sexy for your spouse and that is just Monday! When do we ever get a free moment to ourselves? It seems impossible to just drop everything and take a walk in the park just because we feel like it.

One of my pet peeves, and my wife can attest to this, is to hear people say, "I did not have time to…" Fill in the blank with whatever you "did not have time to do." The reality is you had time, but you did not *make* time to do whatever you did not do. Each of us has the same 24 hours in a day so we all *have* time to do whatever we feel is important that day. Too often we spend too little time prioritizing our most important daily tasks and instead, we fill our schedules until it is bursting at the seams with *stuff*.

We create a busybody lifestyle that overwhelms us with stuff. We are constantly working on stuff or building stuff or filling our minds with stuff, but no real work is getting done. No significant progress is being made on our journey to being a better, more successful leader. I do not think anyone ever completes everything they strive to do in a day, but we must be sure to make time for the important tasks and taking time off is very important and should not be overlooked.

The only way you will ever get time for rest and other enjoyable activities is to schedule time for them. When you are planning your daily tasks, it is important to also schedule your time off. Schedule your down time and your time to relax, relate and release. It has always been difficult for me to simply drop everything I am doing to take a break if my work is not complete. I have found that by scheduling breaks, it prevents me from becoming a workaholic and allows me time to refresh my brain so that I am more effective when I go back to work.

One trick I use to force myself to take "scheduled" breaks when I am writing is to drink a lot of water when I begin. Eventually, the water will run its course through my body, and I will have no choice but to take a break. Those brief breaks allow me to step away for a while and come back with fresh new ideas. It may sound a little bizarre, but it works for me. Are you getting thirsty yet?

Whatever method you choose, be sure to schedule yourself some much needed time off. What good is it to work, work, work if you work yourself to the grave and never enjoy the fruits of your labor? I promise that if you build it right, your business will still be there if you take a day off. The Baby Boomer generation was taught to work hard for 40 years, retire at age 65-70 and live the last 10 years of your life to the fullest. Now many of them are asking for refunds for that false bill of goods they were sold.

Well, I am part of Generation X and we believe that you should work hard until you turn 40, help retire as many future generations as possible and live your entire life to the fullest. *Life* is what we all have been given but *style* is how you choose to live it. You better take time out to smell the rose petals now before you are buried under them only sniffing the roots.

Chapter Takeaways:

_____

_____

_____

_____

_____

_____

_____

_____

_____

_____

_____

_____

How Will I Implement This Lesson?

_____

_____

_____

_____

_____

_____

_____

_____

_____

_____

_____

_____

LEAD 206:
FIND A GREAT WORKOUT PARTNER

Have you ever gone to the gym to work-out and just could not seem to motivate yourself to run one more mile on the treadmill or push yourself to do that one last set on the bench? Then you look over and see a group of guys yelling and screaming at each other "Push it! One More! You can do it!" Even the smallest guy looks like he could beat you in a bench press contest. Then you think to yourself, "How much better would I be if I had some work-out partners like that?"

Improving yourself physically, mentally, emotionally, or even socially is a difficult thing to do. It takes plenty of hard work and dedication making it easy to quit when you are by yourself, and the process gets too tough. Having a great work-out partner to push you through the growing pains and motivate you to get better accelerates your growth and makes both of you better.

For me, networking and meeting new people at functions has always been difficult to do. To just walk up to someone at an event and spark up a genuine conversation before talking business has never been easy for me. I do not have a problem talking to people, but I am more of a straight to the point guy rather than the take you on a tour type. I mean after the "So what do you do for a living?" I'm at a loss. Knowing this about myself, I find it very helpful to take a work-out partner with me to networking events. Having someone who can break the ice and lift some of the conversation burden from my shoulders makes me better in those uncomfortable environments.

When searching for the right work-out partner there are a few qualities he or she must have. First, you both must share a common mindset. You cannot be focused on trying to start your own business with a work-out partner that is counting down the years until they can retire and get their pension. Those are two totally different mindsets and neither of you will grow from that relationship. Secondly, you must equally push one another. There cannot be one dominant partner or one who already has all the answers- that is called a mentor. You and your work-out partner should be on a common journey of self-actualization in some area of life.

Finally, you and your work-out partner must be honest with each other. The only way the two of you will grow is if you agree to be honest with each other about your progress. If you are not carrying your weight or if you are not pushing hard enough, then your work-out partner should have full authority to pull your card and check you without the fear of hard feelings and repercussions.

Finding the right work-out partner may take some time but it will be well worth the effort. You also may have several work-out partners for different areas of your life. My networking work-out partner is not the same as my entrepreneur work-out partner. Understand that your work-out partners and your friends are not one in the same. One or two of them may overlap but for the most part they probably will not.

You may think you have it all together right now but if you want to challenge yourself and become a stronger leader, then you had better find yourself a great work-out partner.

Chapter Takeaways:

_____

_____

_____

_____

_____

_____

_____

_____

_____

_____

_____

_____

How Will I Implement This Lesson?

_____

_____

_____

_____

_____

_____

_____

_____

_____

_____

_____

_____

LEAD 207:
BUILD A STRONG MASTERMIND GROUP

Throughout time it has been said that "Great minds think alike" and "Two heads are better than one." If this is the case (and I believe that it is) then why do so many great minds, try to do everything on their own? There is a term called 'synergy' that is used to describe the greater force that is created when two or more lesser forces combine and work together as one. A mastermind group, advisory board, dream team, think tank, or whatever you choose to call it is a perfect example of how you can create synergy and become a better leader.

Think about how much better a leader you would be if you had a group of like-minded individuals that served as a sounding board on which you could bounce ideas before you moved on them. How much more effective would you be if you ran every strategy through a mental gauntlet of great minds to be picked apart and worked out until the best strategy emerged? That is what a mastermind group allows you to do. It creates that synergy of combining the minds of many to create a bigger, better, fool-proof outcome.

Your mastermind group should consist of individuals from different areas of expertise, but they should all share your common goal. If you are starting a new business, it does not make sense to have a mastermind group made up of five accountants. You would certainly want one accountant, but you would also want people with experience in entrepreneurship, law, marketing, sales, banking, market research, training, and human resources just to name a few. The more areas your mastermind group can cover and work out in the planning phase, the less time you will waste trying to fix mistakes and oversights during the implementation phase.

Weak leaders act from a scarcity mindset. They fear they will be replaced if someone else shines instead of them. They think that their ideas are the only ideas, and their ideas are best exactly how they thought them. No one can improve upon it because it was their idea. They have covered every angle, dotted every "I" and crossed every "T" and they have come up with the one and only way to complete the said task.

Great leaders operate with an abundance mentality. They understand that a sign of a great leader is evident by how many leaders they have developed around them. They believe that there are enough good ideas to go around. They believe that getting the input of a mastermind group is critical to the team's overall success. They believe that they only get better by learning from other people around them.

Chapter Takeaways:

_____

_____

_____

_____

_____

_____

_____

_____

_____

_____

_____

How Will I Implement This Lesson?

_____

_____

_____

LEAD 208:
MAKE YOUR NETWORK WORK FOR YOU

The book *Cracking The Millionaire Code* by Robert G Allen and Mark Victor Hansen deals a lot with increasing your people resources by tapping into your circle of friends and getting them to tap into their circle and so forth. They really blow the law of Six Degrees of Separation wide open. They use an example of you writing down 101 names of people with great centers of influence and getting them to reach out to their 101 people of influence to grow your business.

It blew my mind once I really looked at that thing and understood how powerful that one concept is. Imagine contacting 101 people and just like that getting warm market access to 10,201 people. What if you then asked that group for their list of 101 people? That's over 1 MILLION people that you just gained warm market access to with whom you can share your products, services, or ideas. I don't care what you are into, if you had one million people to support you or to simply listen to your message because their friend recommended you, it would be impossible for you to fail.

You can never again use not knowing people as an excuse for not being successful. Let's say you really do not know 101 people and you only start with 20 people and those 20 people reach out to 20 more people who then reach out to 20 more - that is still 8,000 people. If only 25% of that group believed in what you were doing and became lifetime customers, that would be 2,000 people investing in your business, using your products, and advertising your company to their friends year after year. Even if those 2,000 clients only spent $25 a year with your company, you would earn $50,000 a year. Don't mess around and get them to spend $100 a year. You would be earning $200,000 a year all from just 20 names in your little black book.

This concept has been mastered and used in Network Marketing or Multi-Level Marketing for decades. While some bad companies led by poor leaders have given the industry a bad name there is no denying that this business model works. It is the best way to create leverage for yourself while increasing your income. How long would it take you and how much would it cost you to meet and talk to 1 million new people on your own? The idea of everyone consistently doing a little bit over a long period of time just makes sense.

Each of us is sitting on a gold mine called our phone directory. How much is your little black book worth? Stop letting bank loan denials and credit card rejections put a halt to your dreams. You have access to all the capital you need and you are sitting on generations of wealth if you just take the time to make the list and make the first phone call. Instead of taking out that second mortgage or getting a home equity loan to start your business, start by asking yourself "Who is in my little black book?"

Chapter Takeaways:

_____

_____

_____

_____

_____

_____

_____

_____

_____

_____

_____

How Will I Implement This Lesson?

_____

_____

_____

_____

_____

_____

_____

_____

_____

_____

_____

_____

LEAD 209:
DON'T GET CONSUMED WITH TRYING TO FIT IN

Do you remember as a baby, one of the first toys you received being some kind of shape toy where you had to put the correct shape in the right hole? Mine was a dump truck. Do you remember how frustrating it made you when no matter how hard you tried to force the star shape into the square hole; it just would not fit? You would cry and throw a tantrum because the "toy was broken" and eventually give up and throw the whole truck at your little sister (Sorry, Stacie). I bet if someone were to buy you that same toy for Christmas this year you may ask "What the heck were they thinking buying me this baby toy?" But if that toy is only for babies, why do we as adults still play that same game with our lives?

We try to squeeze our "broke, bad credit, check to check finances" peg into a "lifestyles of the rich and famous" hole by spending more money on a purse than you can afford to put in the purse. Or to appear more well off than we are, we continue to make poor financial decisions. Our youth try to squeeze their "suburbia raised, two parent household, six-figure income, private school educated" peg into a "I'm a drug dealing, high school dropout, gang banging thug from the hood" hole just because that stereotype is celebrated in mainstream media. Constantly we frustrate ourselves trying to fit into something that we are not. We overlook the blessings of what we have and the power of our story, all to fit in with the "in" crowd because we think they have it better than we do.

If you are looking to be a better leader, then you cannot expect to fit in. Followers fit in while Leaders break the mold. In 2008, NFL Quarterback Vince Young was asked to respond to comments made by Donovan McNabb about adversity faced by Black quarterbacks in the NFL. McNabb talked about the extra pressures he faced and obstacles he had to overcome to be judged by the same standards as white quarterbacks in the league. Young stated that McNabb was exaggerating and that he didn't experience the same problems as McNabb. Never mind the fact that Young did not see this as an obvious ploy by the media to quiet the grumblings of a Black player by getting another Black player to say, "it's not that bad." The bigger picture that Vince Young did not grasp is that things for him are not as hard today, because Donovan McNabb came into the league 7 years before him and went through the pain and hardships alone to pave a way for Black quarterbacks, like Vince Young, to be seen as equal to white quarterbacks.

Nowadays, Black QBs are winning league MVPs, breaking passing records, and consistently ranked in the Top 10 of all QBs. But even today, just about every NFL team has at least one Black wide receiver that once played quarterback but was told to change his position because he was not good enough (or smart enough) to lead a team. Had McNabb succumbed to the pressure of "fitting in" instead of proving that Black men can play quarterback and lead a team, quarterbacks like my Baltimore Ravens' QB, Lamar Jackson, may have ended up being a wide receiver instead of a two-time League MVP QB at the time of this publishing. While today many Black QBs are seen as prized commodities and team leaders regardless of race, not too long-ago Donovan McNabb had to prove his worth by leading the pack and breaking the mold.

Chapter Takeaways:

_____

_____

_____

_____
_____
_____
_____
_____
_____
_____
_____
_____

How Will I Implement This Lesson?

_____
_____
_____
_____
_____
_____
_____
_____
_____
_____
_____
_____
_____

LEAD 210:
YOU ARE THE AVERAGE OF YOUR FIVE CLOSEST FRIENDS

The saying goes "You are the average of your five closest friends." Like it or not you are. Think about the cars your friends drive, the places your friends live, the income of your friends, how many children your friends have. If your friends have dreams you probably have dreams. If your friends are positive, you're probably positive. If your friends go to church, you probably go to church. If your friends curse you probably curse. If your friends have negative lifestyles, you probably have a negative lifestyle. If your friends lie, steal and cheat you probably lie, steal and cheat. I think I've made my point. The point is many of us need new friends.

There's another old saying "Guilty by association." Accept it or not, you are judged by the people you hang around. As you begin to grow as a leader you must realize that light and darkness cannot coexist. Some associations you will have to limit and others you will have to break all together. As you grow, your current friends will either grow with you or you will outgrow them. I will let you know now so you are not surprised when it happens, they probably will not grow with you. So, you have to choose what's more important - your current state of reality (underachieving and hanging out with dream stealers) or the possibility of reaching your full potential and meeting better friends along the way.

Don't let your "friends" sabotage your dreams with words like "I'm just keeping it real" or "I'm not being negative I'm being realistic." What's real is what's right now; living check to check, working all day every day to make ends meet, running from creditors, working a job you hate, spending only five hours a day with your family between 6pm and 11pm only to go to sleep, wake up, and do it all over again tomorrow, that is today's reality. Who wants to live like that for the rest of their lives? I don't know any great leader that lives like that. Your dreams of abundant success are not a real possibility to your friends so they feel that it cannot be real for you either. The devil is a liar. If your friends want to "keep it real" by keeping you right where you are then that's a clear indication that it is time to destroy that association.

Chapter Takeaways:

_____

_____

_____

_____

_____

_____

_____

_____

_____

_____

How Will I Implement This Lesson?

_____

_____

_____

_____

_____

LEAD 211:
WHAT ARE PEOPLE SAYING BEHIND YOUR BACK?

A good word goes a long way. As a leader you want people to always speak highly of your leadership aptitude and character in general. They may not always like the things you do or even the way you do it at times, but people should always be able to speak positively about your leadership and respect you as an effective leader. The best leaders do care what other people think about them because they know that each person's perception is that person's reality. In leadership you need people who feel good about you as their leader and trust in the direction that you are leading them.

You cannot be in every meeting, every function, or every event when your name comes up in order to defend your actions when someone speaks negatively about you. You cannot run commercials saying "What I really meant to say was…" Therefore, it is important that you cherish every interaction with others and look at it as another opportunity to spread a positive message about yourself and in turn have those individuals saying good things about you behind your back.

When it comes to getting people to speak a good word about you, every single person matters regardless of their social, economic, or professional status. If I were to ask the last waitress who served you about your kindness and generosity or if I questioned the last "cashier-in-training" about your temper and patience, what would they say behind your back? It is easy to be patient and kind to people whom we feel can help us get ahead in some way or to our family and friends, but how often do you take for granted those seemingly insignificant interactions with everyday folk. You can never allow yourself to jump on your high horse and think that certain people are beneath you and do not matter to your success. You never know what administrative assistant or cashier may be the sister or nephew of a person of great influence. So treat all people respectfully.

Studies have shown that people tell others about a negative experience they had with a company 7 out of 10 times while they only share a positive experience with others 3 out of 10 times. It is hard enough to get people to say good things about you so you must work even harder to be great at what you do in hopes that eventually the word will spread. Having people talk about you behind your back is not so bad, but you better make sure you have given them a reason to say good things.

Chapter Takeaways:

_____

_____

_____

_____

_____

_____

_____

_____

_____

_____

How Will I Implement This Lesson?

_____

_____

_____

_____

LEAD 212:
TAKE A BITE OF HUMBLE PIE

Ask yourself these questions "Do you enlarge others, or do you belittle them?" "Do you feel that you are better than other people simply because you hold a title higher than theirs?" "Are you more concerned with being the Star or the Servant?" Arrogance and leadership are like light and dark. They cannot coexist! The best leaders are those who can look past their title and seek to live a life of service over stardom. Being a leader does not entitle you to mistreat those who follow you, nor does it make you any better than those who call you their leader. The best leaders learn early on that the more people you serve, the more people will want to serve you.

So many leaders allow their inflated egos to get in the way of achieving success. An inflated ego will not allow anyone else to get credit for something you did. An inflated ego will not allow anyone else to feel good about the small task they did if the task you did was greater. An inflated ego also will never allow you to be nearly as successful as you could be without one. Making others feel good about themselves or like they are even more important than you will pay big dividends when it comes to achieving success as a leader. Everyone knows you're the boss. You do not have to keep saying it over and over.

Humbling yourself and learning how to empower others will not only make you a more successful leader but it will make the people you lead more successful. How much more effective would your team be if instead of you always trying to run the show, you began letting members of your team take the lead? The better leaders your team becomes, the better the entire unit becomes. Believe it or not, you are not always right, and your way is not always the best way. When you allow your other assistant coaches, department managers or committee members to step up and lead, it not only makes them better, but it gives you an alternative perspective on a problem and makes you a better overall leader.

Today so many people are caught up in titles and positions. They feel a sense of validation through their title; however, if the title is stripped away what are you left with? There is a saying that says, "Be careful how you treat people on your way up because those are the same people you will see on your way down." How many times have you seen it where an obnoxious boss treats his people any kind of way and eventually the very person whom he treated the worst is promoted to a position above him? It is so much easier to choose to eat your humble pie bite by bite than to be forced to swallow the whole thing at once. Why wait until you are forced to be humble and live with that regret when you can choose to show humility every day?

Chapter Takeaways:

_____

_____

_____

_____

_____

_____

_____

_____

_____

_____

How Will I Implement This Lesson?

_____

_____

_____

_____

_____

_____

_____

_____

_____

_____

_____

LEAD 213:
BECOME A "DREAM GIVER"

One of President John F. Kennedy's most famous quotes was "Ask not what your country can do for you, but what you can do for your country." As a leader your mantra should be "Ask not what my followers can do for me, but what I can do for my followers." Instead of calling yourself "Vice President of Executive Operations", "Senior Chief Management Specialist", "1st Assistant Lord Junior Deputy Master" or whatever new title will be invented this year to make you feel more important than you are; your title on your business card should simply read "Dream Giver." As a leader your sole purpose is to make the dreams of those whom you lead come true. The more dreams you make come true, the more your own dreams will come true.

I would encourage you to take a page out of Walt Disney's book. Walt Disney became a business legend and made his career out of being a Dream Giver. Walt Disney began his animation career during one of the most difficult times in U.S. history, World War II. At a time when tens of millions of soldiers and civilians were losing their lives to war, Walt discovered a way to make Americans dream again. His cartoons lightened the hearts of so many Americans during a tremendously heart wrenching time.

Becoming America's Dream Giver not only helped the people he served but it ultimately helped him as well. As a child, Walt Disney always dreamed of becoming an artist. Today, you would be hard pressed to find someone who has never heard of Disneyland or has never seen Mickey Mouse, Donald Duck or Goofy. Walt realized that if he focused on making other people's dreams come true through his work, he could fulfill his own dreams of becoming a great artist.

What would happen if you became the Walt Disney of your organization? How much faster would your company grow if you focused more on making the dreams of your team come true? The entire Disney business model was centered on making the dreams of the patrons come true. Whether it was movies, cartoons or theme parks, Walt Disney had everyone dreaming about a better life. His Dream Giver attitude was so contagious among his company that even after he died in 1966, his brother Roy carried on Walt's dream to see Disney World built in Orlando, FL.

This Dream Giver mentality has launched Disney into one of the largest family entertainment companies in the world. Even though Walt Disney has been dead for over 40 years, because he sought to make other people's dreams come true, his dream is still coming true today. His story goes to show that "When you wish upon a star" and become a Dream Giver anything is possible.

Chapter Takeaways:

_____

_____

_____

_____

_____

_____

_____

_____

_____

_____

_____

How Will I Implement This Lesson?

_____

_____

_____

_____

_____

_____

_____

_____

_____

_____

_____

LEAD 301:
DON'T TAKE YOURSELF TOO SERIOUSLY

Your ability to have fun and laugh at yourself will prove to have many benefits. Not only does laughter relieve stress but it makes people enjoy being around you. Smiles are contagious and people enjoy being around pleasant people. It has been shown that people also work better when they are happy. As a leader, that joy should flow from the top as you bring a pleasant attitude to work and thereby inspiring maximum performance from your people. Just because you are in a leadership role does not mean you have to be a mean, stoic dictator who rules with an iron fist. There are many different leadership styles, but the most effective leaders are those whom people can relate to and enjoy being around.

Have you ever had a co-worker who was a joy to be around, got along with everyone and never started any trouble and then one day they got promoted to a supervisory role and their entire attitude changed? Suddenly, they could not speak to you anymore or they were constantly finding ways to remind you that they were your new boss. The same person who used to secretly clock you in when you were 15 minutes late for work was now trying to suspend you for coming back 2 minutes late from lunch. Your once cool cubicle colleague got a new title and became the office terror. The same short guy with a great sense of humor got promoted and now developed a Napoleon Complex and would fire anyone who said anything negative about his height, or lack thereof.

These are all symptoms of someone who is taking themselves too seriously. A fancy nameplate on your desk or a private "manager's" cubicle does not change the person you are on the inside. A title does not make you any better or different than you were the day before you got the promotion. If you begin to think too highly of yourself and take yourself too seriously because of a title, then those whom you lead will begin to think less of you and take you for a joke. If being a jerk who rubbed everyone the wrong way did not get you the leadership position, why become that person after you are promoted?

I have always had a problem with organizations that promote the top performers into management simply because they were the top performers. The truth of the matter is, being the top performer yourself and knowing how to teach and develop other people to become top performers are two totally different disciplines. Being a manager and being a leader are not one in the same. In sports it has been said that often times it is the average players who may have ridden the bench that make the best coaches.

While the starters were playing the game, the backup stood by the coach and learned the game. The star players scoffed at the thought of riding the bench while the backups looked at it as an opportunity to learn. After their playing days are over, the backups who did not take themselves too seriously by thinking they were too good to ride the bench find lucrative, long lasting second careers in coaching while the superstar players (who never learned how to teach the game to others) are overlooked and left behind.

Chapter Takeaways:

_____
_____
_____
_____
_____
_____
_____
_____

_____

_____

_____

_____

How Will I Implement This Lesson?

_____

_____

_____

_____

_____

_____

_____

_____

_____

_____

_____

_____

LEAD 302:
WHEN THE REAL LEADERS LEAD, OTHERS WILL FOLLOW

You are only a leader if people are following you. Sure, they may call you "boss", but if your team does not move when you say move then you have gone from being the lead wolf to a lone wolf. You may be doing all the talking but your team is listening to someone else. It may be your name on their checks, but they have attached themselves to someone else's vision. The most humbling experience for any hotshot positional leader is the moment they realize they have lost influence over their team and someone else, having gained that influence, is now leading them.

The real leader holds the power not just the position. Leadership guru, John C. Maxwell calls it the "Law of E. F. Hutton." The "Law" suggests that positional leaders lead the meetings, and the real leaders lead the people. This is why you cannot get caught up with trying to attain a title or a position. This is also why you must understand that regardless of your current title or position you still have the capacity to be a great leader and change people's lives right where you are. Real leaders lead through their actions not just through their words.

The title does not make the leader important; the leader makes the title important. Could it be that the only reason people aspire to hold a high title is because at some point someone who held that title was a great leader? Is it that they have associated the greatness of the leader with the title and in an effort to be great like that leader; they feel they must have the title? Did they overlook the fact that the leader was great before they wore the title and that is why they ultimately received the title? The only purpose a title serves is to publicly confirm that the titled person should have the capabilities to effectively operate in the role of that position.

So how do you become the real leader that others will follow regardless of your title? Maxwell teaches that there are seven cornerstones upon which real leaders are built. One is Character-Who you are. You will draw more followers by the person you are on the inside than by the person you are on the outside.

Two is Relationships- Who you know. The deeper you build your relationships with others the more likely it is they will follow you. Gone are the days of looking at your people as numbers and not caring about them as individuals. If you want people to love following you then you should learn to love them.

Three is Knowledge- What you know. Knowing all the information does not make you a leader but knowing how to properly apply information does. People want to trust that their leader knows how to evaluate any situation, weigh the facts, and come up with the best course of action.

The fourth cornerstone is Intuition- What you feel. Great leaders can see things that others cannot see, make changes, and move forward before others even know what is happening. There are three levels of intuitive leadership: Those who naturally see it, those who are nurtured to see it and those who never see it.

Fifth is Experience- Where you've been. I am all for on-the-job training and trial by fire but if you want to lead others you better be able to show that you have experience putting out fires and overcoming obstacles.

Sixth is Past Success- What you've done. Your track record speaks louder than words. If you can prove that you have been there, done that, then people will be more willing to follow your leadership.

Seventh is Ability- What you can do. As soon as your followers no longer believe that you are capable of delivering on the promises you make, they will stop subjecting themselves to your leadership. The real leader, the leader people will follow, is the leader that can get the job done.

Chapter Takeaways:

_____

_____

_____

_____

_____

_____

_____

_____

_____

_____

How Will I Implement This Lesson?

_____

_____

_____

_____

_____

_____

JUNIOR YEAR

_____

_____

_____

_____

_____

LEAD 303:
ACTIONS SPEAK LOUDER THAN WORDS

This cliché may be ageless, but it is essential in leadership. Has anyone ever told you they cannot hear what you are saying because your actions are speaking too loudly? Do you know people who cry about being broke but still make poor financial decisions? What about people who say they are going to lose weight but eat fast food every day? As a leader your words can quickly become empty promises if your actions do not back them up. Sometimes we are too quick to kick people to the curb when their actions do not line up with their words, yet we quickly overlook when we are guilty of the same offense.

LEAD 303: #ACTIONSSPEAKLOUDER

If we all governed our lives according to the words of other people instead of their actions, we would all be in a hill of trouble. I have lost track of how many people, supposedly serious about writing a book, have approached me, and asked for my advice or help. Most of them expect me to drop everything I am doing right then and listen to a 20-minute synopsis of their great book of poetry and offer them a publishing deal right there on the spot.

Never mind the fact that we are at my book signing and there is a line of people behind them waiting to purchase my book. Their words tell me they would really like to have their book published; however, when I would send them to my publishing website, www.greenehousemedia.com, to follow the manuscript submission process, their actions told a different story since I never heard from 99% of them.

When I was building my network marketing company, I would see countless individuals come to one opportunity briefing or attend one regional rally and leave more excited than they have ever been about the opportunity for a better life. In their ignorance-on-fire state of mind they would shout how they are going to "tear this business up" and how they would be millionaires in six months. All the excitement in the room, the smell of money and the belief that it was not too late to change their future, got them so pumped up that they began to dream again and believe they could be successful. By the next day when it is time to go to work building their million-dollar business, reality begins to kick in and 70% of them enter the witness protection program never to be seen again.

The reality is that if you are truly going to accomplish the dreams you have for yourself then it is going to take some serious committed action and not just mere words. Whether it is getting your book published, building a successful network marketing business or whatever your goal may be; talking about it will get you nowhere. If you want to get the attention of others, then do it with your extraordinary actions and not your eloquent words. Established leaders understand the hard work it took to get to where they are so they will not be impressed with empty promises. They know that there is no substitution for good old-fashioned hard work. If you want to get the attention of the leaders above you, as well as the followers below you, then start by simply going to work.

Chapter Takeaways:

_____

_____

_____

_____

_____

_____

_____

_____

_____

_____

_____

How Will I Implement This Lesson?

_____

_____

_____

_____

_____

_____

_____

_____

_____

_____

_____

_____

LEAD 304:
TAKE ACTION

Think about the many opportunities that each of us is given to change the course of our life. Surely there have been plenty of circumstances that would have redirected our course and outcomes in life had we only stepped up instead of backed up, spoke up instead of shutting up, or showed up instead of given up. Too many people have their best dreams, ideas and life changing events tucked away under a "Not right now" pillow in their mind. If you want to propel yourself into the realm of great leadership then taking action is essential.

The difference between potential energy and kinetic energy is that potential energy is the energy stored up and kinetic energy is the actual energy in action and working. Your potential to become a successful leader is great, however, you must take action, or become kinetic, to access that potential. How much potential you have stored inside is not as important as how much of it you can bring out of you. All your hopes, dreams, promises and plans don't mean a thing if you do not act and work toward them.

It seems simple enough and like it would only make sense, but taking action is really where many weak leaders get hung up. People spend a lot of time and resources making plans, but it takes courage and commitment to put those plans to work. It takes courage to make that first prospecting phone call or to write and implement that business plan. It takes guts to walk away from a comfortable job to pursue something new and uncertain, but taking action is the only way to overcome your fears of failure. I cannot promise you will not fail if you take action, but I can promise if you do not take action, you will fail every time.

God is the Greatest Leader of all, and he has not given us the spirit of fear and yet it is that very emotion that keeps people frozen in the land of "What-Ifs" afraid to step into their destiny. Taking action means you are going to have to get rid of your friends "Shoulda", "Woulda" and "Coulda." Taking action means you are going to have to jump out of your comfort zone. Taking action also means you are going to have to deal with and overcome the bumps and bruises of life. Taking action means you must "Just do it." The bottom line is, if you want to be a better leader then you must DO something.

For anyone to follow, you must first move. You must not only come up with a powerful vision and great ideas, but as a leader, you must be able to act on those ideas and make them come to fruition. Leaders must be able to move from the conference room to completion, from the desk to doing, from ideas to implementation. Leaders aren't celebrated for the great ideas they have; they're celebrated for the great ideas they act on.

Chapter Takeaways:

_____

_____

_____

_____

_____

_____

_____

_____

_____

_____

_____

How Will I Implement This Lesson?

_____

_____

_____

_____

_____

_____

_____

_____

_____

_____

_____

LEAD 305:
DO WHAT YOUR SAY YOU'RE GOING TO DO

The #1 step to holding others accountable is to first hold yourself accountable. Accountability is definitely an area in which you must practice what you preach and lead by example. Let me throw out a few words that in my eyes describe people who simply do what they say they are going to do: Reliable, Dependable, Accountable, Trustworthy, Consistent, Responsible, Faithful and Honorable. Who would not want to have these words describe them? What's stopping people from using those words to describe you?

One of my biggest pet peeves is to see how lightly people take the words they use. People just say things that sound good in the moment or seem like the right thing to say. Unfortunately, they rarely have any intention of carrying out those promises, nor do they have any concept as to how to carry out those promises. If you said you are going to clean it up, then clean it up. If you said you are going to call tomorrow, then call tomorrow. If you said you would love to help me out, then help me out. The power of life and death is in our tongue. Our words have the power to bring forth life as well as the power to bring forth death.

Imagine what your life would be like if every time you said you were going to do something but did not do it, a family member or close friend died. How seriously would you take your words then? Conversely, what if every time you did what you said you would do, a family member or loved one whom you lost came back to life. That is how serious your word is and, figuratively speaking, every day we either kill people or bring life to them by simply doing or not doing what we said we would do. We are all surrounded by the walking dead. People who have lost hope in us, whose dreams we have killed or those who no longer believe, because we did not keep our word and do what we said we would do.

On the other hand, when you begin to hold yourself accountable and do what you said you would do, you will begin to bring life to people. People will be full of hope, joy, and the belief that they can trust you to lead them toward their goals and dreams. It is so easy to just say things without really thinking of the burden of your words and the responsibility you put on your shoulders with every word. As a leader, you never know how much your words and promises mean to the ones for whom you make them. Choose your words wisely and only say it if you really mean it and plan to do it.

I'm reminded of the words of my late grandfather, Howard Makle. He used to get drunk and curse the whole house out. In his drunken state he would yell, "I said what I mean, and I mean what I say, too!" Pop-Pop's ranting did not make a lot of sense to me then, but living those words is an integral part of being a successful, trustworthy leader. After all, who is going to follow a leader they deem unreliable?

Chapter Takeaways:

_____

_____

_____

_____

_____

_____

_____

_____

_____

_____

_____

How Will I Implement This Lesson?

_____

_____

_____

_____

_____

_____

_____

_____

_____

_____

_____

LEAD 306:
HOLD OTHERS ACCOUNTABLE FOR WHAT THEY SAY

"It's OK, don't worry about it." Have you ever told that lie to someone? You know, when someone misses a deadline on a project and leaves you out to dry and you say, *"It's OK, don't worry about it."* Or when someone owes you money for your services and you say, *"It's OK, don't worry about it."* Or anytime you were counting on someone, and they let you down and you say, *"It's OK, don't worry about it."* Let me tell you a little secret. IT IS NOT OK! Every time you tell someone that it is OK to let you down, you devalue yourself not only as a leader but as a person.

Most people might say they try to avoid conflict by just brushing the shortcomings of others off, but I would venture to say you are making things worse by not addressing the situation maturely and holding that person accountable. What good is a team if you cannot count on each player? How effective can you really be as a leader if you are constantly trying to carry the weight of the entire group? If you let people take advantage of you, guess what- they will!

I have been accused of being hard or overbearing at times because I refuse to let people just tell me they are going to do something without explaining to me how they plan to get it done. I have been burned one too many times by people with good intentions but poor execution. I just think it is better that everyone is clear on the expectations and responsibilities of each party at the onset, so then it is easier to troubleshoot any shortcomings. As a leader, when you set your bar high, and people know they must be held accountable for their actions; they know that they cannot just come to you any kind of way without having their ducks in a row. The ability to hold others accountable will ultimately make your job as a leader easier and your group will work more efficiently.

Holding others accountable may cause some growing pains and be difficult in the beginning. Some of your closest friends and colleagues may not be able to handle your leadership growth and your new standard of accountability. You may lose some people who were comfortable letting you carry their weight but once that burden has been lifted, you will be a much more effective leader. You won't win many new friends when you start holding people accountable for doing what they said they were going to do; but leaders don't look to make friends, they look to make people better. And who wouldn't want to be friends with a person like that?

Chapter Takeaways:

_____

_____

_____

_____

_____

_____

_____

_____

_____

_____

How Will I Implement This Lesson?

_____

_____

_____

_____

_____

_____

_____

_____

_____

_____

_____

_____

LEAD 307:
GIVE CREDIT WHERE CREDIT IS DUE

There is nothing worse than putting your all into a project, giving your blood, sweat and tears toward a cause and having great success only to see someone else take all the credit for your hard work. I don't mean the work was done anonymously but rather someone else took credit for the work you did. It's one thing to not receive credit for your work, ideas, or accomplishments and it is another thing to watch someone else take credit for your work. I have served under leadership that has taken credit and gotten the rewards for my ideas, leadership, and insight and it was not a fun place to be. I have never done work to seek attention, but I have never done work as a ghostwriter either.

The spotlight can be a dangerous thing. If you are not careful it will pull selfish behaviors out of you that you did not even know were in you. When people see you as the star they want to invite you to every function, they want to shower you with all the gifts, and they want to scream your name- but what about your team? What about your administrative assistant who answered all your calls and scheduled your every meeting? What about your Vice President who kept all the departments working seamlessly while you played golf on Tuesday afternoons? What about your nameless offensive line that blocked well enough for you to rush for 1,500 yards in a season? When the spotlight is shining on you; that is your time to shine not just for yourself but for all the people that worked behind the scenes to get you there.

No success story was ever written by a lone author. Every success requires the help of many people coming together to achieve a common goal. As a leader, you may not remember every name, but you better not forget that you did not get there on your own. Your leadership role simply makes you the figure head of the greater team. When you are in the spotlight that is your opportunity to deflect the light off you and shine it on your team. Everyone loves to be recognized for a job well done. Besides, by getting in the habit of recognizing your team you will make them all happy and more willing to work with you and for you.

Stop thinking that other people are out to steal your fame. Most people who work behind the scenes are there for a reason. They enjoy the anonymity of their work and are not seeking the spotlight or pressures of being the front man. Giving them credit for their work in a public forum will not threaten your "superstar" perks but may actually increase them.

At any award show you will find award recipients with their "Thank you" list just in case they win. They all seem to understand that while they may be the singer, actor, or athlete whose name the whole world is screaming; they were just a small cog in the much bigger machine that made them. They understand that if they ever want to see that stage again or fill their mantle with any more awards, then they had better give credit where credit is due. If you cannot seem to keep good leaders from leaving your organization or you are struggling to attract good leaders to your team, then perhaps the spotlight is shining too brightly on you. Perhaps you have not spent enough time giving credit where credit is due.

Chapter Takeaways:

_____

_____

_____

_____

_____

_____

_____

_____

_____

_____

_____

_____

How Will I Implement This Lesson?

_____

_____

_____

_____

_____

_____

_____

_____

_____

_____

_____

LEAD 308:
MEET PEOPLE WHERE THEY ARE

The greatest leaders are those who can meet people on their own level. Leaders who can genuinely understand and respect that everyone is at a different place in their lives are able to reach more people. A college senior and a college freshman may go to the same school, but they are not going to be in the same place mentally. A millionaire CEO and a salaried employee may work for the same company, but they are not going to think on the same level. If you want to excel in your leadership ability, then you should start by learning to meet people on their level.

I have always been good when it comes to dealing with children. People often wonder why little children who may be shy and reclusive with other adults open up to me so eagerly. The answer is simple - I meet them where they are. I understand how intimidating it may be for a young child to have a big man over six feet tall hovering over them saying "Coochie Coochie Coo." The first thing I do with a child is kneel to their eye level. I then take off my grown-up hat and put on my little people hat and try to think like they would think. I begin to build rapport and trust with the young person at their level, and then once we have a bond, I can bring them up to my level by picking them up.

Even as adults, people never lose that desire to have someone pick them up. As a leader people are looking, asking, and often begging for you to pick them up. The problem is, those who need the help are often turned off and intimidated by the big six-foot man standing over top of them saying "Coochie Coochie Coo." As a leader you must be able to kneel and meet people where they are before you try to pick them up.

The evolution of my presentation and style came from a desire to meet people where they are. I know that there are millions of people who want more out of life but may have never read a self-help book to learn how to get it. I spent my first decade and a half trying to be like every other self-help guru and geared my work towards people who already enjoyed non-fiction and self-help books. Although my books were very successful and helped a lot of people, I always felt like there was a larger group of people not being reached based solely on the fact that everyone doesn't receive messages the same.

God eventually led me to get rid of the suit & tie and have a lot more fun just being myself and meeting people where they are and easing them into a lifestyle of personal development. Maybe you picked up this book because you thought the cover was hot, or maybe you liked the cover and back copy. Maybe you thought it would be a great gift for someone else and then it really started speaking to you. Whatever the reason you decided to read this book, I am positive that by now you have gotten much more out of it than you initially expected. Hopefully, by me meeting you where you are, your life has improved, and you are on the way to becoming a better leader.

Chapter Takeaways:

_____

_____

_____

_____

_____

_____

_____

_____

_____

LEAD 308: #MEETPEOPLE

_____

_____

How Will I Implement This Lesson?

_____

_____

_____

_____

_____

_____

_____

_____

_____

_____

_____

LEAD 309:
ACCEPT PEOPLE FOR WHO THEY ARE

I want to give you an assignment. I want you to take next weekend off and plan a trip to Florida to visit one of its many orange groves. I want you to pick two dozen of the biggest, ripest, sweetest, orangesty oranges you can find and bring them back home with you. First thing on Monday morning, before you leave for work, I want you to fix yourself a nice pancake breakfast with your favorite breakfast meats, eggs, and hash browns. I want you to pull out those 24 oranges, your juicer, and the biggest pitcher you have. I then want you with as much love as if you grew those oranges in your own backyard to begin squeezing each one into that pitcher and make yourself the best homemade pitcher of hand-squeezed APPLE juice you have ever made.

Does that seem like an impossible assignment? No matter how well the scene is set or how perfect the surroundings are, it is still impossible to squeeze apple juice out of an orange. Even with the best and brightest oranges you cannot squeeze one micro-drop of apple juice out of them. So why as leaders do we try to do that with people? Why do we get so caught up trying to make studs out of duds in our business?

Poor leaders constantly shoot themselves in the foot trying to squeeze something out of people that was never inside of them. You cannot squeeze an administrative assistant out of a top salesperson. You would have a hard time trying to squeeze a 6' 10" power forward out of two parents who are less than 5' 7". And you might be wasting your time trying to squeeze a housewife out of an emergency room surgeon.

Instead of trying to squeeze miracles out of nowhere, excellent leaders accept people for who they are and put them in the best situations to succeed. It is your job as the leader to discover the strengths of your people and use those strengths to benefit the organization. Trying to force people into roles they are not best suited for will only lead to frustration for you and them. You will constantly be running into brick walls trying to put the puzzle together with the wrong pieces and eventually they will get tired of being forced to perform a task which they are not equipped to do.

Once you learn the true character of an individual you must accept the fact that they are that person. You cannot force people to change. People will only change when they are ready to; regardless of the benefits awaiting them for changing. You must avoid getting caught up with trying to save everyone. Some of the greatest potential lies within people who are so blind to the fact that they are special that no matter how you present it; they just will never see it.

Accepting people for who they are does not mean you have to work with them. It simply means you understand that you are not the one who is going to change them. You then must decide if the person they are now, as opposed to the person you want them to be, fits what you are trying to do.

Chapter Takeaways:

_____

_____

_____

_____

_____

_____

_____

_____

_____

_____

_____

How Will I Implement This Lesson?

_____

_____

_____

_____

_____

_____

_____

_____

_____

_____

_____

_____

LEAD 310:
NEVER COMPROMISE WHO YOU ARE

With the competitive nature of business and leadership sometimes you may be tempted to simply settle for good enough or to cut corners to get ahead. As I spoke about integrity earlier in the book, you must never compromise who you are. This does not mean that you never compromise, but you can never compromise your morals, values, and beliefs for the sake of gaining prestige, power, or position. Your inner code of ethics sits at the core of what makes you who you are. If you begin to compromise that code, then you are compromising your entire identity. Once people realize you can be bought by the highest bidder, they'll never trust your leadership and integrity again.

One argument I always try to stay out of is the argument of whether a successful Black person is a 'sell-out' because they either appeal to a non-Black base or they got ahead with the help of non-Blacks. It is hard to tell the heart of people whom you do not know so I usually refrain from judgment and give them the benefit of the doubt. People such as Condoleezza Rice, Oprah Winfrey, Tiger Woods, Michael Jackson, and even Barack Obama are just a few who have been labeled, by Black people nonetheless, as "not being Black enough" at some point in their careers. This is something that has always troubled me because I have been Black all of my life and I still have not found the book *Everything You Needed To Know About Being Black Enough,* nor have I read *101 Ways To Say It Loud, I'm Black And I'm Proud.* Being Black is beautiful...and diverse!

Ever since the first slave ship left Africa, Black people have been forced to compromise who we are. We were forced to compromise our royalty as the kings and queens of the world to be sold as slaves. We were forced to compromise our ancestor's names and take on the names of our slave masters. We were forced to compromise our family structure by being sold on the auction block to the highest bidder. We were forced to compromise our education by acting like we were dumb and could not read. We were forced to compromise our dignity by enduring the Jim Crow Laws of the South. We were forced to compromise so much just to survive that far too many of us have no clue anymore as to who we really are.

But even through all that our forefathers still fought so that we could have a brighter future. Today we have more opportunity than ever to make a positive impact on the rest of the world and yet we waste time fighting with one another over our Black Card status.

I know all about the temptation to compromise just to fit in with the mainstream. The pressure to grab a seat at the table weighs on us all at some point. But once I began saying "Eff your table! I'm building my own!", I felt so much freedom to just be unapologetically great at being ME. Too often, we will shun those who are begging us to serve them and would willingly follow us, all because we're chasing approval from another group who isn't even checking for us, but we feel somehow validates us more.

One of my favorite biblical quotes has always been "What does it profit a man to gain the world but lose his soul?" Whenever I'm faced with a decision where my integrity and character are on the line, I ask myself that question. If I can't live with the answer, I turn down the offer. Sure, I could probably be ten times as rich and famous as I am now had I chased certain opportunities, but where would my soul, peace, and mental health be? I am who I am and if that's not good enough for someone, then they weren't for me to impact anyway.

In leadership it should not matter what race you are, but you must strive to reach and help as many people as God blesses you to reach. It is more important that you find and stay true to yourself rather than getting caught up trying to hit an acceptable mark on some fictitious sliding scale of validation from any one group. A leader must be willing to stand firm on his or her beliefs, be willing to defend them against the toughest opposition, and most importantly, never compromise who you are for anyone.

Chapter Takeaways:

_____

_____

_____

_____

_____

_____

_____

_____

_____

_____

_____

_____

How Will I Implement This Lesson?

_____

_____

_____

_____

JUNIOR YEAR

_____

_____

_____

_____

_____

_____

_____

_____

LEAD 311:
GET PAID FOR WHAT YOU KNOW, NOT FOR WHAT YOU DO

One important long-term investment every leader should make is an investment in education. I don't just mean formal school education but ongoing personal development and an investment into your mind for your entire life. Once your mind has been expanded it is impossible to shrink it back. It should be every leader's desire to learn as much about their field as possible and become an expert in it. The more you know the more valuable you become. That's why you want to move from getting paid for what you do to getting paid for what you know. You will always get paid more for what you know than for what you do.

How many times have you worked a job where it seemed as if you did all the work while your boss sat in their office doing seemingly nothing, but they got paid more than you? Think about it, who gets paid more, the professional athlete or the team owner? Most professional athletes have played their sports all their lives, playing that game is all they have ever done and may be all they know how to do. The small percentage that reach the professional ranks are paid handsomely and live great lifestyles.

The team owner on the other hand, more likely than not has never even played the sport of the team he or she owns but they know how to run a business. They know how to organize and run a profitable company and fit the many pieces together to make a successful organization. The athletes get paid for what they do, and the owner gets paid for what they know. Even LeBron James makes less than The Buss Family who owns The Lakers.

No matter what the field the same holds true. In education, the teachers get paid for what they *do,* and the principal gets paid for what she *knows*. In music the singers get paid for what they *do,* and the label executives get paid for what they *know*. Even lawyers and doctors get paid for what they *do,* and judges and the surgeon general get paid for what they *know*. So, if you want to get paid more you must *learn* more, not do more. Instead of doing more like working 10 hours overtime, use that time to learn more, get a promotion, and earn more.

Most people who complain about their job never say they hate what they *know*, they always hate what they *do*. I don't care what it is you do; your job knows they can always find someone else that can do what you do, but can they find someone who knows what you know? Ever wonder why companies always downsize management and labor but never layoff the Sales or IT Department? It is a lot more difficult to replace knowledge than it is to replace laborers. If you want more long-term success, job security and you want to invest in your future, always strive to get paid for what you know and not for what you do.

Chapter Takeaways:

_____

_____

_____

_____

_____

_____

_____

_____

_____

_____

_____

How Will I Implement This Lesson?

LEADERSHIP UNIVERSITY

_____

_____

_____

_____

_____

_____

_____

_____

_____

_____

_____

LEAD 312:
FINDING YOUR NICHE WILL MAKE YOU RICH

What gifts do you possess? What special talents or skills do you keep hidden in your back pocket? Finding what you are good at and allowing that gift to manifest itself in your life could be your ticket to abundant success. Finding your niche and mastering it can lead not just to financial riches but to riches such as peace, happiness, joy, and fulfillment. It is easier to prosper when you begin to develop that special gift in you that God designed just for you as opposed to trying to master something that was made for someone else.

Finding your niche as a leader is also important. What is it that will set you apart from other leaders in your field? What makes you special and stand out? Are you a vocal leader or do you lead by example? Are you a dynamic speaker or an eloquent writer? Are you good at motivating the masses or do you excel in one-on-one coaching? Maybe you have a knack for conflict resolution or perhaps you are a great negotiator. Knowing where you fit into the mix helps you to put yourself in the best environments and situations to succeed. Finding your niche and becoming an expert at it will open doors to leadership that would have stayed locked to you otherwise.

When it comes to leadership, being an expert in a field or two is the goal. Being a jack of all trades is the worst nemesis of leadership. Great leaders understand that they cannot be all things to all people so they build a team of people around them who can fill the needs of the people. Great leaders find their niche and perfect it and surround themselves with leaders who have perfected their own niches in other areas. The stronger the leaders you surround yourself with the more you can develop your own niche.

Part of being a leader means being able to understand your strengths and weaknesses and allowing the right people who are strong where you are weak to stand in the gap for you in those areas. Believe me when I tell you that if you are a leader who feels you must do everything yourself and you know everything about everything then don't worry because you will not be a leader for long. You will one day look around and ask, "Where did everyone go?" You will soon see that people don't stick around long with know-it-alls. Once you find your niche, it is important that you empower others to find and develop their own niches.

If you desire maximum success in all you do then you must find your niche, master it and watch the riches flow. You want your name to be the name people call when they are searching for an expert who does what you do. Once you find your niche and become great at it, the people will start talking and success will surely follow.

Chapter Takeaways:

_____

_____

_____

_____

_____

_____

_____

_____

_____

_____

_____

How Will I Implement This Lesson?

_____

_____

_____

_____

_____

_____

_____

_____

_____

_____

_____

LEAD 313:
IT'S EASIER TO SELL SOMETHING YOU'RE PASSIONATE ABOUT

Among other things, leadership is a sales job. A leader must sell a vision to those whom he leads. Selling any intangible item is difficult, but selling something that does not even exist should only be attempted by professionals. So how does one sell something and get others to buy-in to something that they cannot put their hands on and for most, cannot wrap their minds around? You must stop trying to sell your idea and start selling your passion.

The Encarta Dictionary defines passion as "An intense or overpowering emotion. A strong liking or enthusiasm for a

LEAD 313: #SELLYOURPASSION

173

subject or activity." Your passion for your vision, your cause, your idea should be so intense that it overpowers all naysayers and negativity. Your passion and enthusiasm should be infectious and contagious. When you are passionate about something people will be drawn to your visionary leadership and be begging to work with you.

When you are passionate about a dream, you think about it day and night. When you are passionate about a dream, you excitedly tell anyone who will listen about your ideas. When you are passionate about a dream, that excitement drives you to act toward it every day. When you are passionate about a dream, you don't take "No" for an answer. When you are passionate about a dream, other people feed off that and become passionate about your dreams as well.

It's not hard for preachers to sell salvation when they are passionate about it. Their passion is evident in their commitment to the word they preach and the lifestyle they live. It is that very passion that intrigues and draws people into the church and gets them excited about finding their own passion for salvation. It's not difficult for an author to sell books when they are passionate about their work. Their passion is evident in their excitement and the fervor with which they hustle to sell books. Many readers buy books simply because the author was so excited when they told them about the book that the reader just had to buy the book to find out more.

As a leader it should not be difficult for you to sell your vision if you are passionate about it. Your organization should see your zeal and your intense emotion toward fulfilling your goals and be moved to join you. You can avoid the leadership pitfall of wondering why your team doesn't get excited and respond to your call to action by maintaining a high level of passion for your dreams and visions. When you are passionate, it makes selling the dream that much easier. If you are great at selling your passion for your dream, the word will spread, and the people will come.

Chapter Takeaways:

_____

_____

_____

_____

_____

_____

_____

_____

_____

_____

LEAD 313: #SELLYOURPASSION

How Will I Implement This Lesson?

_____

_____

_____

_____

_____

_____

_____

_____

_____

_____

_____

LEAD 401:
HAVE A "BOTTOMS UP" MINDSET, NOT A "BOTTOM LINE" MINDSET

Since I brought up network marketing, let me talk about it here as well. One of the most pressing questions network marketing representatives receive is "Is this company a pyramid scheme?" Most people look at the industry as a system that scams people because all the little people at the bottom do all the work while a small number of people at the top get paid all the big money. While any reputable network marketing company has a compensation plan in place that rewards the people who work the hardest over those who simply joined the company first; the pyramid model is not that much of a foreign concept.

Think about your own job. Do you work for a company where there are a lot of bottom dwelling employees doing all the work and the CEO gets the most money? Did you know that on average, a CEO for a Fortune 500 company earns 40 times more than his employees? That sounds like a pyramid scheme to me, yet no one walks into their job yelling "This is a scam!" What about our government? Don't we have one Chief Executive over top of Representatives of the people and on the bottom are all the neglected people? Does that mean our government is a pyramid scheme? Is our country operating a scam?

The pyramid structure itself is not the problem but it is the mindset behind it that is troubling. Corporate America, which in essence *is* America, has always been run with a *Bottom-Line* mindset. Employees do not matter, customer's health and safety do not matter, the environment does not matter, and fair competition does not matter, only the bottom line and how much money the company makes matters. Movies such as *Boiler Room* shed light on the business world's philosophy of winning at all costs and sticking it to the little guy. Companies such as Enron, Tyco and MCI Worldcom were run by leaders with a *Bottom-Line* mindset, and they left their employees high and dry all in an effort to fill their own pockets.

I believe businesses would see much longer lasting and fulfilling success if more of them adopted a *Bottom-Up* mindset. This business philosophy understands that every business is standing not on the shoulders of their overpaid CEOs but on the shoulders of their grossly underpaid employees. When leaders begin to put the best interest of the employees before their own interest, they can see far greater results and growth. When you look at a pyramid, the largest part is at the bottom. The large base is what gives the pyramid its strength and that is the same in leadership. Your people are your base and your strength so it would be wise of you to think of them first in all you do. Do not stop caring about those below you simply because you made it to the top.

Chapter Takeaways:

_____

_____

_____

_____

_____

_____

_____

_____

_____

_____

_____

How Will I Implement This Lesson?

_____

_____

_____

_____

_____

_____

_____

_____

_____

_____

_____

LEAD 402:
DON'T LET THE BELIEF LEVEL OF OTHERS LIMIT YOUR DREAMS

If you have friends who are constantly dissuading you from going after your dreams then it's time for you to find some new friends. We all have fallen victim to sharing a dream that excited us with a friend or relative only to have them shoot it down for some reason. Sometimes those friends may have valuable insight and justification for shooting it down but most times, if those friends aren't experts in the area of that dream, all they're really doing when shooting down your dream is telling you that your dream is too big for THEM.

Pledge today to never again forfeit your dreams because it is too big for people in your circle. Rather than forfeit your big dreams, forfeit those small thinking friends for the time being and go after your dreams! Once you achieve your dreams, those people will either come back around or you'll meet better bigger thinking new friends along the way. It is not your responsibility to make sure your friends are comfortable with your dreams. It IS your responsibility however to make sure you passionately and vigorously pursue your dreams. It IS your responsibility to provide the best lifestyle possible for your family.

Your friends don't mean any harm. They really think they are helping you by warning you of the dangers of chasing your big dreams. The reality though is they are projecting their fears and uncertainties onto your ideas, and you have to be wise enough to recognize when that happens and strong enough to stand up against it when it does. The bottom line is we don't pick our friends first based on their expertise in the areas important to our lives. We pick them on compatibility. Since we don't pick them based on any level of expertise, then why do we so often let our non-expert friends dictate to us what plans for our lives are best?

Here is something that I had to painfully learn firsthand. Do not expect your family and friends to be as passionate about your dreams as you. That was a difficult pill for me to swallow when it was forced down my throat. But it is not their fault. I had to learn that while my family truly loved me, they only knew one side of me. They only knew the family, Ryan. The hang out and have a good time, Ryan. None of them really knew the business Ryan, so it was difficult for them to just jump on board when I began sharing all my dreams with them.

I remember when I was publishing my first book *Success Is In Your Hand* and I sent out a letter to 30 family members requesting financial assistance to publish my book. I needed $5,000 to cover printing the books and marketing materials, so I figured that would be a cinch to raise between 30 households. My heart was broken when I received only one check in the mail from my cousins in Petersburg, VA. While I was very grateful for their support, I could not stop wondering what happened to everyone else. I knew there was no way I could have sent the letter to 29 wrong addresses so why did my family not support my efforts?

Your family and friends may not "get it" in the beginning, but that doesn't mean they do not like you or that they do not wish to support your efforts. Sometimes they are just looking at you through tainted glasses. They know too much about the "right now" you to see you as anything other than what you already are. The thought that there may be a greater purpose for your life other than making potato salad for the family reunions is too hard for some to grasp.

Most people spend their lives building the perfect box to put them and their family in and when someone close to them decides to bust out of their box it can be frightening. Your family loves you without a doubt. They think they are trying to stop you from getting hurt by discouraging you from living outside of their box. The only way to overcome that doubt and make believers out of your family and friends is by going out and having massive, supernatural, extraordinary success. Remember, it is your dream, not theirs. The difficult truth is it's not their responsibility to support it.

Chapter Takeaways:

_____

_____

_____

_____

_____

_____

_____

_____

_____

_____

_____

_____

_____

How Will I Implement This Lesson?

_____

_____

_____

_____

SENIOR YEAR

_____

_____

_____

_____

_____

_____

_____

_____

LEAD 403:
QUIT GRINDING AND START BUILDING

Words are important. They manifest in our lives whether we want them to or not. So, the words we choose are critical to our success. I'm going to share a peeve of mine with you. I hate the word "GRIND" when it's used to describe one's journey toward pursuing some dream or building a business. I used to use it just like everyone else. You hear people talking about being "on my grind" or "out here grinding" or sometimes it's used to encourage others like "Keep grinding" but one day it hit me- grinding is not fun.

Think about your goals and what you're trying to accomplish as a leader. Think about the lives you want to impact, the greatness you want to achieve, and the legacy you want to leave. Think about how long you've been "on your grind". Now, look at the word "grind". Grind means to "reduce down into small particles". Do you see that? When you grind something, you are actually breaking it down into small particles. You're not actually building. To grind is the opposite of building. Can you think of a single positive image that correlates with grinding something? Do people even smile when they express their journey as "the grind"? Usually not. It's time to put that word to rest and start BUILDING.

To "build" means "to construct by putting parts together over time upon strong foundation". Look at that! Isn't that what leadership is about? Putting parts together over time upon a strong foundation. When you grind two bricks together it creates dust and the bricks crumble. However, when you build with bricks, you create the strongest type of structure. "Foundation" is "the lowest load bearing part of building which is typically unseen." The foundation bears the weight of the building, it's the unsexy part no one sees but without it, the entire building would collapse. Too many leaders and organizations have great skills, products, services, and talents but they lack foundation. They're steady grinding or trying to build upon a weak shaky foundation.

Here are six cornerstones I want to give you for building a strong foundation:

SCOPE

Your scope is the mission and purpose of your venture. Why are you doing it? Who do you plan to reach? What impact do you hope to have? You must know all of this to direct your actions.

SUPPORT

Who is going to support you as you build? You need to know who is on your Team. That could include employees, advisors, vendors, other experts. Then you need your Mastermind Group. These are people who may not be actively helping you build your project but are offering counseling and expertise along the way. They are your sounding board of experts. Then you need your Doers. These are the people who are going to bring your vision to life. They're the ones, well...doing. Finally, you need Ambassadors. These are your cheerleaders to the public. These are the ones giving you reviews on sites, spreading the word on social media, and doing your word-of-mouth advertising for you.

SYSTEMS

A System is something that does the job the same way every time. The more automated the system the more productive and profitable you will be. If you don't have great systems in place, your business will suffer as you ultimately fall behind, lose track of clients, lose sales, and always work harder than you need to work. A few systems you should consider are CRM to handle your clients. You need to have one place where the info and correspondence for all your clients is housed. No more sticky notes and lost business cards. You need a sales system. You need to have a proven way to go about making a sale in your business. This shouldn't be left up to chance. You need a product delivery system. Once an order is made how will you deliver the product or service to the client? What is you marketing system? Do you have a true automated marketing system or are you simply throwing stuff out there with no real plan and hoping it sticks? Finally, what is your follow up system? If the fortune is in the follow up, then you can't leave your fortunes to chance. Implement systems that ensure you never forget to reach out to a client when you're supposed to.

SCALABILITY

Every business leader desires massive growth. No real leader is comfortable with "just enough". But here's a little secret: You must be ready to handle growth BEFORE you grow. You can't wait until you get on *Shark Tank* and THEN try to upgrade your website to handle the traffic. You can't wait until you get an order from a big box retailer for 20,000 units to start looking for fulfilment avenues. Even as you're only closing 3 or 4 deals a week, even as you're the only employee, you should be building your organization NOW to handle the growth you hope to have.

SELF-AWARENESS

Know who you are and be THAT! Your foundation must be built upon a genuine, authentic, totally sold-out version of YOU. You can't get caught up trying to be everyone you see. You must know who you are and be true to that person. Don't allow every success story you see online to dissuade you and get you trying to change directions every 6 months. Make your plan, focus on that plan, and work that plan. The saying "Stay in your lane" is great advice when it comes to remaining aware of your own abilities, strengths, weaknesses, and superpowers. You can never be better at being someone else than they are at being them. All you can focus on is being the best You.

SUSTAINABILITY

Are you building to last over the long haul? Anything worth building is worth having around for a while. The final cornerstone for any foundation, as a matter of fact, the very purpose of any foundation, is to ensure that what you're building is going to be around for a long time. As you lead others and build your organization, you should always build from a sustainability mindset. Ask "Is what we're building going to be around for the next 100 years if we keep building it this way?" If you can't answer that question affirmatively, Tweak the plans and try again. Leaders aren't interested in building "here today, gone tomorrow" fly by night organizations.

Chapter Takeaways:

_____

_____

_____

_____

_____

_____

_____

_____

_____

_____

_____

How Will I Implement This Lesson?

_____

_____

_____

_____

_____

_____

_____

_____

_____

_____

_____

_____

LEAD 404:
STOP USING YOUR CIRCUMSTANCES AS YOUR COP-OUT

So, you're looking at your present life and you're not happy. In your mind life sucks right now and it's all because of your current situation and circumstances. You feel like you can never move forward because of how bad things are right now for you. Guess what my response is to that? "SO WHAT?!" Starting today "So what?!" needs to also be your response to your current circumstances.

For years you have allowed your past to have rule over your present while simultaneously sabotaging your future and enough is enough. Let today be the last day you allow your circumstances to be your cop-out. Your past failures and missteps can no longer be the reason why you can't achieve your goals but let them be your motivation for why you MUST achieve your goals. Every successful leader has some situation or mistake they made that they could have allowed to hold them back. The difference is those people decided to use their stumbling blocks as stepping-stones into their greatness.

Maybe you have a criminal record. Maybe you have a track record of poor relationships. Maybe you have been a piss-poor parent. No matter what your challenge has been, no matter how much society tells you that you cannot succeed because of it, make today the day you decide to no longer be bound captive by the dark cloud of your mistakes and shortcomings. Decide today that YOUR story will be the story of the one who overcame despite it all.

As a leader, people following you are expecting you to encourage them and help navigate them through tough times. If you always let your circumstances get in the way of your success, how effective do you think your organization will be once your team starts doing the same thing? We all face challenges, but very few of them are truly so insurmountable that quitting is our only option. When trouble comes knocking at your door, stop letting it move in and reside in your life. Evict that trouble by saying "So What!" and keep pushing anyhow.

It's easy to look at your current situation and accept that you cannot live any better than you are because of the cards stacked against you. But truly great people, abundantly successful people, don't take the easy road. Stop accepting your self-imposed excuses that allow you to live a mediocre life and begin today to press for a higher mark right from where you stand. Decide today that you will never use your current situation as a cop-out again.

Chapter Takeaways:

_____

_____

_____

_____

_____

_____

_____

_____

_____

_____

How Will I Implement This Lesson?

_____

_____

_____

_____

LEAD 405:
SHIFT FROM DREAMS OF DESPERATION TO DREAMS OF DESTINY

God has designed each of us for a specific purpose. He has put in us everything we need to fulfill the purpose He has for our lives. Whatever it is He has called you to achieve in life, He has already paved the way for you to walk in that purpose. The problem most people face, however, is finding out just what that purpose is. For some like me, God's purpose for my life was made clear to me. For others, they struggle with discerning between their passions and God's purpose for their life.

Then there are your dreams. Your dreams are man-made. They come from your own passions, desires, and talents. Your dreams consist of the goals and accomplishments you wish to achieve throughout your lifetime. You are free to develop your own dreams. Your dreams hopefully line up with your skill set or else they may be unrealistic dreams. If you are in tune with your purpose, your dreams most likely line up with that purpose and run in tandem. God knows what He's purposed for your life but He's not going to purpose you to do or be something that doesn't excite you. You won't dread living in God's purpose for your life.

Then there is destiny. That place where your dreams meet with God's purpose for your life is that place called "DESTINY". When your dreams are coming true and they line up with God's purpose for your life, that is the magnum opus, the epitome of success, the high life. When you can wake up every day doing what you love to do and know it's also what you were created to do, that's when you know you are living your best life.

Now that you know what destiny is why would you want to experience anything less than that level of living? For most people, me included, who are struggling to break through to a new level of success, one big factor holding them back is the level of their dream. When you dream from a survival mindset you can only dream of getting by. You can only dream as big as making ends meet and saving the little you already have. Those are Dreams of Desperation.

Dreams of Destiny allow you to dream bigger than your current situation and see yourself the way God sees you. Dreaming from a Destiny Mindset allows you to open your mind to dream as if you already are the person you were purposed to be, and you are simply waiting for the manifestation of those dreams. You are simply waiting for and working toward the outward confirmations of the inward declarations.

Believe me I understand what it feels like to have nothing and all you can think about is surviving through the month. That's a terribly dark place to be, let alone try to dream about anything more than which bill collectors aren't going to extend you anymore grace periods. A life of lack is depressing. It makes you feel less than human and even dirty at times. However, what I've found is that when you're broke, no matter if you dream big or small at that moment, you're still broke. So why not dream big, see your life from a destiny perspective and launch from there?

That doesn't mean you live in some fantasy world and ignore all that's going on around you. What it does mean however is you release the hold all those material things have on you by accepting that if you lose them now, it's not the end of the world and that simply makes room for new things and opportunities. If you found a way to acquire them once, you can find a way to acquire them again. Your current season of lack is just a proving ground for your time of destiny. How you operate now with little shows God how you will act with much. Never give up on your destiny simply because you are currently struggling.

Chapter Takeaways:

_____

_____

_____

_____

_____

_____

_____

_____

_____

_____

How Will I Implement This Lesson?

_____

_____

_____

_____

_____

_____

_____

_____

_____

_____

LEAD 406:
MAKE PEOPLE R.A.V.E. ABOUT YOU

The best form of communication when it comes to you growing your personal brand is 3rd party verification in the form of mouth-to-mouth endorsements. You want to be that person everyone raves about when your area of expertise is brought up. You want to position yourself as the go-to person in your field. Here are four qualities you must have to make others R.A.V.E. about you.

RELEVANCE- The first thing you must bring to any relationship and communication is relevance. There must be a need for you and your message. If you are an expert on picture tube televisions in the current world of flat screen HD LED TVs then you are irrelevant. It doesn't matter how much you know about your subject, if it has no impact on present matters then no one will listen. One big pitfall "experts" fall into is not being able to keep current with their industry so that their message remains relevant and needed.

AUTHENTICITY- People can smell a salesman a mile away. They can smell authenticity too. I believe it's OK to be a copycat just as long as you're copying the right cat but stop trying to be like everyone else. Find your own voice and message that speaks to you first before you try to share it with everyone else. Don't worry about being the best [insert what you want to be here]. Only concern yourself with being the best YOU. Don't get caught up with every new Flavor of the Month that comes along. Stay true to yourself and let your authenticity sell you.

VALUE- There's an entire chapter on creating more value in this book but understand that the more value you bring to a relationship, the more difficult it is for others to replace you. If you focus on being more valuable by being the best at what you do, then people will have no choice but to rave about you to others. Don't be overly concerned with what you're getting out of every interaction. Instead concern yourself first with how much value you're bringing to the interaction.

EXCITEMENT- Here's a little secret- The more excited you get about whatever it is you're talking about; the more excited people will be to listen. It's like magic; only it's real. Excitement is contagious! If you want folks to get excited, you must get excited first. More times than not people will follow your excitement before they even follow your words. While you're spending all that time crafting the perfect message, make sure you spend enough time crafting the perfect delivery as well.

So, for the million and first time, "Communication is Key". Know what you are saying out of your mouth as well as through your body language and actions. Take charge of your message and convey it the way you intend to. Say what you mean to say! Mastering the art of communication will not only make your life better but the lives of those to whom you're communicating better too. If you want or need more out of life, you need to know how to communicate that need to those who can give it to you.

Chapter Takeaways:

_____

_____

_____

_____

_____

_____

_____

_____

_____

_____

_____

How Will I Implement This Lesson?

_____

_____

_____

_____

_____

_____

_____

_____

_____

_____

_____

LEAD 407:
TREAT PEOPLE "AS IF..."

How would you treat someone today if you knew that 10 years from now you would have to ask them for $10 Million Dollars? Would you be so quick to curse them out when they upset you next time? Would you smear their name all over social media sites for the sake of "keeping it real" to get revenge for something they did to you? How you respond to and interact with people today could have huge impacts on your life in the future. There's an old saying about not burning bridges because you never know when you may need to cross them again and I wish more people thought about that before they went flying off the handle.

For me, it was my first radio interview being by someone I had a positive interaction with 12 years prior. For you it may be a former co-worker who ends up being HR Director at a company you're applying to 10 years from now. That singer you kicked out the group without so much as a phone call and explanation could end up becoming Program Director at the very station you've been trying to get to play your new single. Your ex-girlfriend could go on to become a doctor and deliver you and your current wife's baby (happened to me TWICE). You just never know how things are going to go so it's important you treat each person as if they are potentially a decision maker on a $10 Million deal for you.

This doesn't mean you go around using people and building fake relationships in hopes of getting a big payoff in the future. What I'm saying is focus on building genuine relationships and treating people with the respect you would hope to be given. Control your emotions in uncomfortable situations so that they never come back to bite you and prevent you from bigger and better things down the line. The instant gratification of getting something off your chest right now may ultimately prevent you from future success you seek down the line.

God tells us "That which you do the least of them, you do also to Me." How are you treating the "least of them"? Sure, it's easy to show respect to the current decision makers and bosses who hold your future in their hands. But how are you treating the janitors and secretaries you pass by on your way to your corner office? Do you treat waitresses like they owe you something and you're doing them a favor by allowing them to serve you in restaurants? How do you treat people when no one else is around?

How would you treat people if you began to act as if they were the most important person in YOUR life at that moment? It doesn't take much effort to make someone's day. All it takes is a willingness to humble yourself and genuinely want to see someone else experience joy. We all get angry and peeved, we all get cut off in traffic, we all get lied too, or let down, but what if that was literally God on the other end of your meltdown? Would you still "just have to get it out"? As you lead yourself and lead others, begin to "act as if" that person has the key to your future in their hand and your response will determine whether you are elevated or not.

Chapter Takeaways:

_____

_____

_____

_____

_____

_____

LEAD 407: #TREATPEOPLEASIF

_____

_____

_____

_____

How Will I Implement This Lesson?

_____

_____

_____

_____

_____

_____

_____

_____

_____

_____

_____

LEAD 408:
LEARN TO FORGIVE

I truly believe that a super majority of the pain, heartache, stress, and drama people experience in their lives is there simply because they have not learned to forgive. People spend more time focused on someone else doing them wrong and seeking revenge on that person over their hurt than they spend focused on figuring out how to simply let it go and move on. Forgiveness is your most powerful weapon! The freedom attained from simply letting go is life changing. Past pains have no power once you have truly forgiven the inflictor of the pain.

For some reason people have come to equate forgiveness with weakness. They seem to feel like forgiving someone means you've lost the battle. I look at forgiveness as the exact opposite. When you can forgive someone for the hurt they caused you, you negate any power they once had over you. The minute you quit harboring negative feelings and energy over their actions you gain freedom and victory.

If GOD can forgive each of us for the plethora of sins we commit daily, and still love us enough to sacrifice His only Son so that we may still have everlasting life with Him in Heaven, then who are you to think you cannot bring yourself to forgive that humanly person for ANYTHING they may have done to hurt you? Get over yourself and get to forgiving! Forgiveness doesn't mean you allow someone to continue hurting you, but it does mean you've released the grip their transgressions once had on you. We humans are always the first to expect forgiveness and second chances when we mess up but will find any and every reason we can to rationalize why someone who hurt us isn't worthy of that same forgiveness and second chance.

Stop letting simple arguments ruin great relationships. All people really want to know in an argument is "Did you hear me and did anything I said matter to you?" If we spent less time yelling and more time listening during discussions of disagreement, we would also spend less time mending broken relationships. Sometimes arguments happen, not because someone is trying to be right, but they are simply trying to be heard. They're tired of being ignored and having their voice lost in the noise. They want to know that they matter to you.

When you can learn to shut up and listen to the other voices in your relationships and value those voices as much as your own, you will find your relationships begin to grow exponentially deeper as others become more comfortable in trusting you with their thoughts and vulnerabilities. As a leader, you are going to have people let you down, you are going to have people mess up, but you must be quick to forgive and coach them along. True leaders can build relationships, even with people they may not get along with, as opposed to kicking every person they disagree with out of their lives.

Chapter Takeaways:

_____

_____

_____

_____

_____

_____

_____

_____

_____

_____

_____

_____

How Will I Implement This Lesson?

_____

_____

_____

_____

_____

_____

_____

_____

_____

_____

LEAD 409:
PEOPLE ARE YOUR MOST VALUABLE ASSET

I don't know how many times I've said it in this book but if you haven't figured out by now that people are the most valuable resource you can access, you should start over reading from Chapter 1. There's no getting away from that fact. None of us live in a vacuum or inside of our own self-contained bubble. We need each other to survive and thrive so how we relate to one another is most important. The more people you have on your team, in your circle, at your disposal, the more valuable YOU are to others. Why do you think every author wanted to be on Oprah's Book Club List? Why do people make such a big deal over how many

Twitter Followers people have? Why are companies like Klout sprouting up to rank your social media influence? It's because you're only as valuable as the people you know.

There is a caveat though. Knowing people isn't good enough. How those people feel about you is where the true value lies. You can roundup thousands of people who will at least pay attention to what you have to say, but if you don't touch them or make them feel like more than dollar signs in your eyes, then you just lost those same thousands of people. You must touch people and build real relationships, real connections. We live in the day and age where we send mass text messages for everything from holiday greetings to birth and death announcements. Try this novel idea- call instead of text. You may be amazed at just how impactful that once normal gesture can be on building relationships since it's now out of the norm.

The minute you begin taking people for granted you will begin to see your relationships suffer because of it. Don't focus so much on quantity but make quality your goal. It's much easier to get $10 out of one happy client 10 times than it is to find 10 new clients to give you $10 each. Foster your relationships and give even more than you receive. Before you ask someone to do something for you, first find something you can do for them. No one likes a leech that uses people for money grabs. You be the person to others that you want others to be to you.

Relationships don't have to be difficult if you keep a few things in mind:

1) Only get into relationships with people you genuinely care about.

2) Be open and honest within your relationships.

3) Be fair and equitable, not expecting more than you are willing to give yourself.

4) Know when it is time to end relationships no matter how good or bad it is.

5) Understand that you cannot get into every relationship presented to you.

6) Loyalty in relationships is the top priority.

7) Allow room for personal growth among those in the relationship.

Keep these tips in mind and you will be creating better relationships in no time.

Chapter Takeaways:

_____

_____

_____

_____

_____

_____

_____

_____

_____

_____

_____

_____

How Will I Implement This Lesson?

_____

_____

_____

_____

_____

_____

_____

_____

_____

_____

_____

_____

LEAD 410:
DON'T LET YOUR CIRCUMSTANCES CONTROL YOUR CHARACTER

"Character" is defined by Merriam-Webster as: the mental and moral qualities distinctive to an individual. It's the distinctive nature of something. Character is a noun. Character doesn't describe you, like an adjective. Character isn't something you do, like a verb. Character is a thing. It is what and who you are. Your character is your distinct nature. It is made up of what you do, how you think and what you believe is right and wrong to make up You. Your character speaks for you when you are not around to speak for yourself. Your character is what drives your actions and decisions. Aspects of your character may change over time but your character itself is permanent.

Merriam-Webster defines "circumstances" as facts or conditions connected with or relevant to an event or action. It's an event or fact that causes or helps to cause something to happen typically something undesirable. So, our circumstances lead to certain events and actions. Negative circumstances don't necessarily lead to negative events, just as positive circumstances don't always lead to positive events. Circumstances change like the wind. We cannot always control our circumstances, but we can, and must, control our responses to all our circumstances. Circumstances are temporary. Character shouldn't be.

As you embark on your leadership journey, it is important to realize and accept that your circumstances right now are just what's going on right now. You cannot allow your temporary situations to affect your permanent character. Do not grow impatient during the process of creating a better you and end up going against your character by taking shortcuts that could lead to even worse results.

Emotions are not a bad thing, but allowing your emotions and how you feel in the heat of the moment to determine how you respond to circumstances could have much farther-reaching consequences on your future than you can fully evaluate at that time. No matter the circumstances, always lean on your character as your guide when it comes to making the proper decisions. You control your circumstances; don't let your circumstances control you. Before you act, follow these steps:

Evaluate your goals and how they pertain to each decision. Things may not always go the way you desire, however if you understand your goals, you have a better chance at making decisions that will be best for you even if they hurt a little bit.

Weigh all possible outcomes. Taking time to evaluate outcomes prevents you from making emotional and impulsive decisions. You can quickly eliminate options that do not line up with your goals for the particular scenario.

Think about how your decision will affect others. It's a selfish person who only puts their needs into consideration when making any decision. If your decision will negatively impact those closest to you then that may not be the best choice to make.

Decide which consequences you are willing to live with. Whether it is a criminal not thinking about the years behind bars they'll spend if they get caught or the cheating spouse not thinking about the lifelong repercussions from creeping with a jump-off for even one night, if you can't live with the consequences of your decision don't choose that path!

Choose to do the right thing. "Right" doesn't necessarily default to morally right (although that's preferred) but what is right for you and your situation based on the assessment you made during the decision-making process. You can never go wrong by choosing to do the right thing.

Chapter Takeaways:

_____

_____

_____

_____

_____

_____

_____

_____

_____

_____

How Will I Implement This Lesson?

_____

_____

_____

_____

_____

_____

_____

LEAD 411:
LEAVE A LEGACY

Some people are destined to be the lead singers while others fit best in the role of backup singers. Some people relish the role of being the team's leading scorer while some are content being the 12th man on the end of the bench. If you have read all the way through this book, then I guess it's safe to assume you want to be a lead singer. You want to make a bigger impact in the world and make sure everyone knows you were here. My question for you then is what are you going to leave behind?

In the musical *Hamilton* there's a line that says, "Legacy is planting seeds in a garden you will never see." When your work here is done, what are you going to leave behind to make sure people know you were here? We all leave something. What we leave is the true indicator of the legacy we've left, and the story others will tell about us. The overwhelming majority of people spend their lives declaring their love to their family and friends and when they die, they leave the people they love nothing but bills and debt. Nothing says "I Love You" like bill collectors calling your family after your death to collect debts they didn't even incur. How about trying something different and leaving the world something else to remind them you were here?

How about leaving some Works? What tangible evidence of your existence will you leave behind? How many books are going to die with you that you should be writing right now instead? How many of your songs will people be singing long after you've departed this life? How many homes will you build? What kind of clothes will you design? How many movies will you direct? There must be something in you that you could be doing right now instead of continuing to push it off. Get to work on whatever it is you were designed to create and make it happen before it's too late.

Maybe you have ideas you plan to leave behind? I know I've invented at least 4 products in my head that I never did anything with. What about you? Maybe your idea is also an invention. Or maybe you have come up with a more efficient way to achieve some tasks. Wouldn't it be great to have a process or law even named after you? Start putting those ideas on paper and begin working out a plan to put them into action. They won't do you any good in the grave with you so you might as well share your great ideas with the world and make your mark!

Here's a new idea. How about leaving some money? Yes, leave some cash for others. Billionaires like Bill Gates and Warren Buffet have gotten so rich over their lifetimes that their new goal is to give as much money away as they can. You may never reach billionaire status, but you have your entire life to work on creating income generating assets that will continue to either pay your family or whomever you decide to donate your wealth to once you go. It doesn't take millions to start a scholarship fund at your college alma mater in your name. The one thing about money I've learned over time is the more willing you are to give it away, the more room you will make to receive even more. Even if you have nothing more than a life insurance policy, that is much better than leaving the bill for the funeral behind.

Lastly, what about leaving people? A true success story of legacy isn't about how good you were, it's about how good you were at duplicating your success in the lives of others. True legacy is all about the crew of leaders you develop along the way. When you leave who is left to carry the torch? That's the essence of legacy. When you have built people up to be even better than you and continue your work once you're gone, that creates a living legacy for years to come. Build up others and you can live forever.

The best thing about being alive is that as long as you're living, you can start over every single day. Every day is a new beginning

LEAD 411: #LEAVEALEGACY

towards creating the life you were purposed to live and cementing a legacy you and your family can be proud of. If your daily focus stays on becoming a better leader, then your positive legacy will grow in lockstep with your efforts. You cannot force people to regard you in the way *you* would like them to regard you so don't get caught up focusing on how every action is going to affect your legacy. You can't write that part of the story yourself. You just remain focused on doing the right things and helping the most people and when you are gone, they will write the story for you.

We are living in a world today that's the result of the actions of others decades, even centuries ago. We are the personification of their legacies. The world we see today is a product of the actions they made years ago, and our lives are better or worse for it. What are people going to say about you 50 years from now? Just like we're standing on the shoulders of those who sacrificed for us 50 years ago, there will be people 50 years from now standing on the shoulders of your work and contributions to society. The decisions you make today will determine whether they're standing with smile or a frown.

Take charge of your legacy right now by simply deciding to make your life about more than just you. Decide today that you will be the one in your family tree that everyone else is thanking for changing the family's fortune and destiny. Make a choice that you will be the one to break the generational curse of financial lack in your family. Why can't you be the first one to graduate college and create a legacy of greater educational expectations in your family? It doesn't take much to change the course of your life and thereby change your legacy. However, it does require sacrifice and commitment. It's up to you to decide if it's worth it. Are you going to strive to make an unforgettable mark in the world while you're here or just pass away like you never existed?

Chapter Takeaways:

_____

_____

_____

_____

_____

_____

_____

_____

_____

_____

How Will I Implement This Lesson?

_____

_____

LEAD 412:
NEVER GIVE UP

In 1969 The Baltimore Colts faced the underdog New York Jets in the NFL's Super Bowl III. The New York Jets were led by a young Joe Namath and were the inferior AFL team. Many were shocked when Joe Namath guaranteed a Jets victory over the Colts. The Colts were coached by Don Shula and were the clear favorites to win. That game went down as the "Greatest upset of all time" as the Jets defeated the Colts 16-7. After the loss, Don Shula was ridiculed, practically blacklisted, and ultimately fired by the Colts.

Surely dejected and feeling down, Don Shula could have quit coaching, but he didn't. Don Shula went on to coach the Miami Dolphins where he went to three straight Super Bowls, won back-to-back Championships in 1973 and 1974 and led the Dolphins to the only undefeated season in the history of the NFL. The coach that was once ridiculed and suffered the greatest upset of all time went on to win more games than any other coach in the history of the NFL and is known as one of the "Greatest Coaches of All-Time."

For Don Shula quitting was never an option. Even when everyone was against him and told him he did not have what it took to succeed, he believed in himself and became more successful than any other coach in the history of the NFL. Quitting cannot be an option for you either. No one is going to give you success on a silver platter. You are going to have to scratch and claw to get it. You are going to have to believe in yourself when no one else does. As a leader you have the destinies of all your followers in your hand. If you quit, then you not only forfeit your destiny, but you forfeit the destiny of everyone following you.

There is a price to pay for success but when it is all said and done, there is also a price to pay for failing. If you apply the lessons taught in this book, the only thing that can stop you from becoming a great leader is you quitting. As one of my mentors used to say, "It is impossible to stop a man or a woman who will not quit." Too many lives are attached to your success and leadership. There are people that are waiting for you to finish your race for you to help them through their own. When you quit, you are not just quitting on yourself, but you are quitting on all the people depending on you to press on.

What would have happened if Michael Jordan would have quit playing basketball after he was cut from his high school team? What would have happened if Bill Gates quit playing with computers after he dropped out of school? What would have happened if Oprah had quit talking when people told her she was too fat to host a show and that she could never beat Donahue? What is going to happen if you quit because the road gets too rough? *"When the road you're trudging seems all up hill and cares are pressing you down a bit, rest if you must but don't you dare quit."*

Chapter Takeaways:

_____

_____

_____

_____

_____

_____

_____

_____

_____

_____

_____

How Will I Implement This Lesson?

_____

_____

_____

_____

_____

_____

_____

_____

_____

_____

_____

_____

LEAD 413:
STOP WANTING IT AND START WALKING IT

When it comes to your dreams and being successful, are you WANTING it or are you WALKING it? Far too often people spend their lives talking about their dreams and never spend enough time walking their dreams. It's easy to dream the dream and want it to come true, but the part that separates the great leaders from the average ones is the ability to walk in it and do it!

You can either wait for your ship to sail in or you can jump in the water and swim out to the ship! Wanters aren't bad people, they're simply misguided. They have fooled themselves into thinking they're working their dreams but if they were truly honest with themselves, they'd admit their efforts aren't really going toward business building activities. They may be in the neighborhood but they're not actually on the right street. Wanters may call themselves XYZ but they aren't actually DOING XYZ. For instance, you may say you're walking as a professional speaker, but if you're not actually doing speaking engagements and constantly working to book engagements, then you just WANT to be a speaker. Simply having a website up promoting you as a professional speaker and hoping by some grace of God, a company finds you and books you, isn't walking it, that's wanting it.

Here are some more differences between those who want versus those who walk:

THOSE WHO WANT	THOSE WHO WALK
Get business cards made	Hand out business cards daily
Build their website	Market their site to build traffic
Call themselves "XYZ"	Do the things an "XYZ" does
Come up with great ideas	Make great ideas come to life
Quit when things get tough	Go harder when things get tough
Listen to naysayers	Their work shuts up naysayers
Play around on social media	Build brands on social media
Act alone	Build teams
Procrastinate	Act with urgency
Make and accept excuses	Ignore excuses

What happens when you waste time only wanting your dreams to come true? Opportunities will pass you by. If you're sitting on the sidelines watching, it's impossible to throw the winning touchdown. Opportunities don't go away; they simply go to other people. Wanting will have you sitting home watching other people capitalize from your great ideas. Wanting will also make you get mad at the success of others who are walking. You start to try and find any excuse as to why that person must have done something other than actually work hard to achieve their success. Your anger at their success is really you being angry at yourself for not walking your own dreams. Finally, it can leave you depressed. Depressed at the idea that you know you were gifted with so much talent, yet you simply sat on it and let it go to waste.

On the flip side, here's how walking in your dreams manifests in your life. Doors of opportunity will begin to open. When you're actively working, people who need your work will easily find you. Opportunities begin to fall in your lap. Sometimes just being in the right room, with the right people, at the right time, will bless you with opportunities that would never have come otherwise. That's how I ended up on stage with speaking greats Willie Jolley, Delatorro McNeal II, Cheryl Wood, Che Brown, and Kim Coles at one event. They needed another speaker, and I was there.

When you're walking it, your creativity begins to surge. There's no greater stimulator of creativity than working on solving a problem. When you're working, you begin to see all kinds of new avenues and alternatives. You begin to see things you would never have seen had you still been on the sidelines. The game looks totally different when you're on the field. Finally, when you're walking it, success begins to overflow. Momentum is the greatest force for any business. It's the one thing every leader seeks. The caveat is you must actively be moving to create momentum. Walking it is the only way to ever gain the momentum you seek.

So, from this day on, it's time to be honest with yourself and stop wanting to be something and begin walking as that thing. Begin to DO what it takes to be it and watch your life and your leadership change forever.

Chapter Takeaways:

_____

_____

_____

_____

_____

_____

_____

_____

_____

_____

_____

How Will I Implement This Lesson?

_____

_____

_____

_____

_____

_____

_____

_____

_____

_____

_____

LEAD 414:
START SETTING S.T.U.P.I.D. GOALS

Let's talk about setting goals. Unless you've lived under a rock your entire life, or unless this is your first time exploring the world of professional development, then you've undoubtedly set goals. But not only set goals, you've probably seen or been taught something called S.M.A.R.T. goals. S.M.A.R.T. goals are cool but leave out a few important criteria when it comes to setting goals you will actually achieve.

S.M.A.R.T. is an acronym for Specific, Measurable, Action-Oriented, Realistic, and Time-sensitive. This is a great place to start and build your foundation for your goals but even in using this framework, far too many goals still go unachieved. That pushed me to look deeper into goal setting and I created something I've termed...wait for it...S.T.U.P.I.D. goals! S.T.U.P.I.D. goals is also an acronym and I believe that once you add these six components to your goal setting, these will be the missing pieces to setting goals that are impossible to quit! I've recorded a full audio training on Setting S.T.U.P.I.D Goals available at www.settingstupidgoals.com that you can download for free. This training will go deeper into it, but for now, in the space I have, I will give you a quick sneak peek into what S.T.U.P.I.D. goals mean.

SACRIFICE: The S is for Sacrifice. Too often when setting goals, we focus on the outcomes and how life will improve once we hit our goal. What I've found is we often overlook the journey and what demands achieving our goals will have on us. When setting goals, we must be honest about what sacrifices are necessary for us to reach our goals. When you're honest and confront this upfront, you are shocked when that sacrifice needs to be made because you've already prepared yourself and everyone else impacted by it for the sacrifice.

TEAM: The T is for Team. I know we all think we can do it all ourselves, but that's not how success works. When it comes to achieving anything great, it takes a team of people to get it done. There's a saying that goes, "If you want to go far, go alone. But if you want to go fast, build a team." See, you may eventually have success as a solo show, but the name of the game in today's world is speed! Build yourself a competent team and accelerate your success.

UPLIFT: The U is for Uplift. Who or what is being uplifted by your goal? Just like I started this book asking, "Who is at the center of your why?", if your goals are only about you, it will be much easier letting yourself down than if others are depending on your success. Be clear on what the bigger mission of your goals are and that will help you press towards them when the road gets tough.

PLAN: The P is for PLAN. I've discussed the importance of having a plan a few different times in this book, so I don't need to spend too much space here rehashing it. But understand that a goal without a plan is merely a dream. You must spell out in as much detail as possible what your plan is to reach your goal.

INCENTIVE: The I is for Incentive. There are two questions I think you should ask yourself as it relates to incentives when setting goals. The first question is "What does it cost to not show up and achieve your goal?" It's easy to imagine what the reward will be when you achieve your goal but being clear on the cost of not achieving your goal, and deciding if that's a price you're willing to pay is just as vital. Secondly, ask yourself, "How will you reward yourself for hitting your goal?" Yes, the goal itself is rewarding, but reaching the finish line and being disciplined enough to finish shouldn't go unrewarded.

DAILY ACTIVITY: D is for Daily Activity: Don't fall into the trap of setting a goal and then making a long laundry list of to-dos for the goal. The winning formula is to set daily activities that if consistently done, will lead to you achieving your goal. So, no matter what your goal is, be clear on what you must do daily to achieve it.

Chapter Takeaways:

_____

_____

_____

_____

_____

_____

_____

_____

_____

_____

How Will I Implement This Lesson?

_____

_____

_____

_____

_____

CAPSTONE COURSE

_____

_____

_____

_____

_____

_____

_____

LEAD 415:
GET COMFORTABLE BEING IN ROOMS THAT MAKE YOUR UNCOMFORTABLE

I've heard it said that your level of excellence can only rise to your level of exposure. So, what does that mean? Think about it. Have you ever thought you were doing OK for yourself? Thought you were doing great and living your best life. Then you met somebody else who was just living life at another whole level than you and left you like, "Oh, my God, I had no idea that level of life was even an option!" Only because you were never exposed to something different.

That's what I want to challenge you with in your leadership and life. Expose yourself to greater levels of excellence. Expose yourself to higher levels of excellence where you're not even sure you belong yet. Put yourself in rooms that you don't feel comfortable in because of the level of excellence that's in that room. Once your mind has been expanded, it's impossible to shrink it back. That exposure will shift what you see as "normal". It will challenge you and push you to raise your level of excellence so that you become comfortable in that room. You'll not only begin to believe you belong there, but you will long to be there. Your old rooms will now make you uncomfortable because you've outgrown them.

I look at the last several years and how much I invested in just putting myself in rooms and spaces around people who were at higher levels than me, people who knew more than me, people who were willing to sow into me and the quality of life those experiences gave me. Being in those spaces, while I may have felt uncomfortable at first, positioned me to overcome any imposter syndrome I may have felt, believe even more in my abilities and purpose, as well as made me more confident that I could help those I serve achieve more just like I did.

When you find somebody who's doing something better than you, don't hate on them. Don't sit there and be jealous of them. Find out how they did it. Find out how you can connect with them. Sit down with them (even if you must pay them). Ask them pertinent questions that will help your growth journey. Sit at their table until you are ready to build and invite others to your own table. It's not a bad thing. Upgrade your level of excellence by upgrading your level of exposure.

CAPSTONE COURSE

You cannot expect to effectively lead others to higher heights and expose them to greater possibilities if you haven't walked that same walk yourself and felt that same fear and discomfort they feel. Those who follow you will buy into your belief as their form of down payment on their own belief. Don't be out here fronting and leading your flock to slaughter because you have them believing in you and you're just teaching something you believe but haven't been exposed to our experienced yourself.

Chapter Takeaways:

_____

_____

_____

_____

_____

_____

_____

_____

_____

_____

_____

How Will I Implement This Lesson?

_____

_____

_____

_____

_____

_____

_____

_____

_____

_____

_____

LEAD 416:
SOMETIMES IT'S OK TO QUIT

Hey, I know in business everyone is always like, "Go! Go! Go!" But the question I get all the time is, "When is it okay to quit?" Never! You must never quit. You gotta keep going! Go down with the ship! You cannot give up! Nah, I'm playing. Yes, you can. Newsflash! Sometimes, it is OK to quit. I know this is an unpopular opinion because every personal development coach will probably tell you to never quit. Shoot, keep reading this book and I'm going to tell you the same thing! But sometimes quitting is acceptable. Sometimes quitting is not quitting. It's just changing. It's what we call making a pivot. Here's two key indicators to help you determine when it's OK to quit.

The #1 indicator that it may be time to quit is: You have reached the capacity of learning any new information in what you do. I mean you literally cannot learn anymore. You can't take in any more information on the subject. You have learned all you can possibly learn about what it is that you want to do. Whether it be because you have exhausted all the information there is to learn or you are exhausted by all the information there is still to learn, if you have hit your wall of understanding, then it may be time to move on. Once you stop growing, you're dying. If you know Algebra is as much as your brain can process, then forcing yourself to learn and apply Calculus is a bad move for everyone involved.

The #2 indicator that quitting may be a good idea is: You have no desire to learn anymore. If you've already learned everything and maxed out at what you can or want to learn from a situation and have no desire to learn anymore, then OK, it's time for you to move on to something else. There's no reason for you to be there unless you just want to be the know-it-all in the room. But no one likes know-it-alls, so why would you ever want to be that?

So, those are the two times I believe quitting is not just OK, but probably the best idea. When you have maxed out your capacity to learn and when you no longer have any desire to learn anymore, that's when it's time to quit. That's when it's time to move on. But I want to be clear on one thing. When I say it's OK to quit, I'm not talking about totally quitting on your dreams and purpose. I am speaking specifically to knowing when it's OK to quit on the path you're taking or the means by which you chose to pursue your goals and dreams. It takes a strong, humble, and insightful leader to look at their situation and circumstances and say, "Yeah, this ain't it." It takes a lot to be able to admit when you've maxed out and squeezed all the juice there is to be squeezed out of a situation. But the sign of a strong leader is their ability to recognize those times and effectively pivot without losing the confidence of their team.

Chapter Takeaways:

_____

_____

_____

_____

_____

_____

_____

_____

_____

_____

How Will I Implement This Lesson?

LEAD 416: #ITSOKTOQUIT

_____
_____
_____
_____
_____
_____
_____
_____
_____
_____
_____
_____

LEAD 417:
MAKE YOUR LEADERSHIP MATTER!

You do not need a title to be a leader. However, if you do have the title, do your best not to suck at it. Too often, people treat leadership like it's their favorite dessert. Everyone craves the dessert, but no one wants to eat their Brussel sprouts first. There is a lot that goes into being a great leader. All of it isn't fun or even enjoyable. Sadly, having the title of leader doesn't automatically impart you with the wisdom to effectively lead. Being a leader is sexy. Who wouldn't want to experience the swag that comes with leadership? However, while the best leaders make it look easy, they all know just how difficult leadership can be.

I bet if you were to survey 100 people in leadership roles and asked if they considered themselves to be great leaders, 80-90% of them would reply in the affirmative. But the truth lies with those whom they lead. If you were to survey their direct reports and ask them if their leaders are great at leadership, I'd venture at least half of those leaders would be surprised by the responses they receive. We have all worked for horrible leaders, as well as seen horrible leaders at work. With America's 45th president, we witnessed exactly how dangerous inept, inexperienced, and immoral leadership can be to a country and a world. Poor leadership has an exponentially negative impact on those being led. Therefore, it is imperative you understand the impact your leadership has and not take your role for granted.

I want to share three quick points about the Top 3 Reasons Leaders Fail. I did an entire training on this in an episode of The Passionpreneur Podcast so I will share the abridged version.

Reason #1: Leaders fail because they are color blind. In my position as the Director of Marketing and Development for a former nonprofit employer, during a meeting with an employee, we were reviewing a spreadsheet of potential donors. I was expressing to him what our game plan would be and how we would approach differing donors. As I was talking, I would give him directions like "Everyone highlighted in green will get a letter and every name in red needs to be removed from the list." The more I spoke, the more befuddled his countenance became. Eventually, I asked him what was confusing him. It was then that he informed me he was color blind. He couldn't discern all the colors on the spreadsheet! All the organizing and segmentation that made the data clearer for me, had subsequently made it far more ambiguous for him. After that, we figured out a better way to get the job done that fit his skillset better.

Fortunately for that guy, he had a great leader. Ha! But how many times do leaders make the mistake of assuming everyone on the team sees things the same way? Breakdowns from poor communication often stem from leaders assuming everyone "gets" what is being said, because it makes sense to the leader who said it. Never considering that subordinates who don't understand will more likely remain quiet about it rather than risk looking like they aren't qualified. The most impactful leaders take time to ask questions, listen to feedback, and adjust their own communication when necessary.

Reason #2: Leaders fail due to their inability to take decisive action. When is the best time to buy a smoke detector? When everything is fine, or while the house is on fire? As a leader, you cannot wait until your organization is burning to install smoke detectors. As I coach on impact leadership within organizations, one constant complaint I hear regarding organizational culture is teams who complain that their leader doesn't take decisive action when it comes to nipping potentially culture destroying employee behavior in the bud. We have all been there. We have all worked in environments where every single employee knows who the problem child is and they all but beg the leader to handle that person, yet the leader inexplicably ignores, or even worse, enables said behavior. I have watched an entire management team walk out the door because of how the Executive Director failed to admonish, and even rewarded poor performance from certain employees while fostering a culture of mistrust and backstabbing.

Your team expects you as their leader to take decisive action. If your team brings a problem to you, as their leader, they expect you to make the decisions and take the actions they cannot take. Failure to address negative culture breeds resentment amongst employees towards you as the leader. Your failure to act when necessary, will cause you to lose your best people. You cannot allow one deadbeat to jeopardize your integrity as a leader and expect your team to ride for that. Stop ignoring the smoke detectors in your organization warning you of problems. Once you allow an inferno to rage, there is no rebuilding the destruction you accepted. No one is going to want to hear your suggestions and bright ideas on improving things after watching you allow the whole thing to burn while ignoring their alerts of danger.

Reason #3: Leaders fail because they lose the trust of their team. Do you know what I have the most difficult time getting leaders to do? Let me spare you the guessing game. Leaders have the most difficult time admitting they made a mistake. I don't get it. Leadership does not equate to perfection. No one in their right mind expects their leaders to never make mistakes. I'd venture that if you aren't making mistakes as a leader, you aren't as impactful a leader as you may think. But you know what is even worse than making a mistake as a leader? Lying about it. No one trusts a liar. Your team will forgive your mistakes if they trust you. The minute you give them reason not to trust you, it's a wrap.

As I write this section, I am coming to realize one fact. I have really worked for some terrible bosses! But I digress. The point I want you to takeaway is, if you find yourself at the point as a leader where you are covering up more than you are sharing and spending more time making excuses than executing, just save everyone the added stress and leave. Once your team no longer trusts you to lead them, while they may not physically leave, they have already checked out mentally and planning their escape. You see it in sports when a team starts losing. The owners don't replace the stars, they replace the coach. They bring in a new voice to reach the players. It's the same game and same players, yet somehow the team starts winning. The change was the team's renewed trust in a leader and their willingness to go all out for a leader they trust.

Chapter Takeaways:

_____

_____

_____

_____

_____

_____

_____

_____

_____

_____

_____

_____

How Will I Implement This Lesson?

_____

_____

_____

_____

_____

_____

_____

_____

_____

_____

_____

_____

FINAL EXAM
10-STEP LEADERSHIP GAME PLAN

Now it's time to go to work. Throughout this book I have given you 52 weekly leadership lessons. Now it is time to bring it all together by giving you a game plan to put into action that which you have learned. All of what you have learned is worthless if you do not have a game plan for implementing it into your life. I have given you the playbook and now here is the game plan to unlock the successful leader within you. There are 10 daily action steps that will serve as your plan of action to ensure your success. This game plan combines aspects of the yearlong leadership training with easy to do behaviors that will get you started right.

10-Step Successful Leadership Game plan

1. Decide To Be Successful
2. Discover Your Vehicle
3. Develop Your Strategies
4. Duplicate Someone Who Has Already Done It
5. Daily Positive Affirmations
6. Daily Personal Development
7. Desire To Be The Best You Can Be
8. Destroy All Doubt
9. Don't Waste Time
10. Don't Ever Quit

1. Decide To Be Successful

Your first step is to make the decision to be a successful leader. No one ever says they want to fail but millions of people make that decision every day. Making the decision to be successful is more than simply saying you want to be successful. It requires a resolve within you to be willing to go through the journey necessary to reach success. Deciding to be successful also means you refuse to allow any negative forces and influences to penetrate your positive mental being. No one is going to force you to be successful. You have the power to choose what kind of life you will live. Whether you realize it or not, every decision you make is either a decision to be successful or a decision to fail.

How you spend your time, money and resources are all decisions you make to either fail or succeed. Decide to be successful by making successful decisions.

2. Discover Your Vehicle

Success is not some hocus pocus mojo where you just sprinkle some magic pixie dust and voila, you're everything you want to be. Success takes work. You must put something in to get something out. Therefore, you need a vehicle that will serve as the platform for your success. By vehicle I don't mean a plane, train, or automobile but your occupation, profession, or vocation. Your vehicle is simply what you do that garners your success. Selecting the right vehicle is extremely important to your success. It is so important that God has already selected it for you. You simply must ask Him to show you and direct your path toward it.

Don't fall into the trap of trying to be successful in a field that you were not purposed for. Someone else's success in any given area does not guarantee yours. Your vehicle may be education, entrepreneurship, writing, singing, mechanics, cleaning, preaching, accounting or any one of millions of professions. The key is to discover YOUR vehicle. Once you discover your vehicle, then expand it and maximize it. Explore every opportunity available within your vehicle. Figure out how you can get the most out of what it is you do, how you can impact the most lives through your vehicle, and how you can help and empower the most people coming up after you.

3. Develop Your Plan and Strategies

Once you have discovered your vehicle and your goals, it is time to make your plan and strategy. There is a familiar saying, *"If you fail to plan, you plan to fail"* which proves that your plan is very important in reaching and achieving your goals. Another saying goes, "A goal without a plan, is simply a dream." Could you imagine your favorite sports team taking the field and the coach telling the players to just figure it out and play? Every pro sports team has great players, but why are some more successful than others? Often the differentiator between being good and being great is one team's plan and strategy for the game. The best coaches are those who also know how to adjust their strategy on-the-fly. What do you think "Half-time adjustments" are? Every successful leader has goals as well as strategies to achieve them. Be purposeful about your strategy because success does not happen by accident. There's no such thing as an overnight success. Success comes from making a plan and working the plan.

4. Duplicate Someone Who Has Already Done It

What is the easiest way to get what you want? Find someone who has already *ethically* done it and do what he or she did to get it. In school we were always taught to do our own work and not to copy. We were punished and called cheaters for getting help from someone more skillful than us. But in the real world "cooperative learning" will get you a lot further a lot faster. I was once told, "It's OK to be a copycat just as long as you copy the right cat". I'm not talking about cheating or stealing from others but I'm talking about finding mentors and other successful people who are willing to share with you what they did to become successful.

Why do you think the ABC show *Shark Tank* is such a huge hit? Millions of people audition for a chance to become business partners with billionaire sharks. Every contestant knows getting a deal with a Shark is the opportunity of a lifetime. How much faster could you reach your goals if you had the Marc Cuban, Lori Greiner, or "Mr. Wonderful" of your industry teaching you step by step how to do what he or she did to become successful? I spent six years in undergrad and grad school and amassed over $100,000 in student loan debt because I wanted to learn how to start and run my own business. Imagine how surprised and dismayed I was when I realized that all my instructors had PhD at the end of their names but not one had CEO. Don't misunderstand me, I received a great education, I just feel I could have gotten a much better, and less expensive, business education from business owners. A mentor can accelerate your growth and guard you from the pitfalls that they have already experienced. A man that findeth him a mentor has foundeth him a good thing.

5. Daily Positive Affirmations

What better way to begin and end each day other than reciting positive daily affirmations to yourself? The world will feed you more than enough negative thoughts and images to process and discard each day. You must take personal responsibility for feeding positive thoughts to your mind. I can promise you that every day will not go as you planned and sometimes life will flat out stink. So, who is going to pick you up and urge you to keep going? Who is going to be the good angel on your shoulder saying, "You can do it"? Who is going to pick you up from the muck and mire called life? You.

It is your responsibility to monitor what goes into your mind daily. The best, time-proven method to maintaining a positive outlook on life and developing high self-esteem is speaking positive affirmations to yourself on a regular basis. One time here and there is not going to do it. It must be a regular behavior that becomes second nature. The more you speak it, the more you believe it. The more you believe it, the more you become it. The more you become it; the more success becomes you.

6. Daily Personal Development

"The more you know the more you grow." I don't know if that's an old saying but it should be. Keep in mind that you can only get out of you what you have already put in you. See yourself as an empty bank account in need of a daily deposit. The more deposits you make the more valuable you become. Personal

Development is like your Rainy-Day Fund; you never know when you will need it, but you feel much more secure knowing it's there. Personal Development improves not just your knowledge but also your confidence, ability, and skill level. It helps you become a better person and prepares you for your inevitable success. Your position in life today is a direct result of decisions you made five years ago. Where you end up five years from now will be determined by the decisions you make today. Make the decision to invest in daily personal development and watch what happens five years from now.

7. DESIRE TO BE THE BEST YOU CAN BE

This book is designed to help you become the best leader you can be. It does God, the world and yourself no good for you to just be OK, average, or good enough. The world is saturated with average people that are just good enough. Millions of people take their untapped gifts and talents to the grave never knowing what could have been. Successful leaders desire to be the best they can be. Do not get tripped up in trying to be the best but push to be the best *you* can be. Being the best you can be has nothing to do with anyone else. You are not competing with anyone but yourself to be the best you can be. Being the best you can be means when it is all said and done and it is time to take an inventory of your life, you can honestly, without a doubt, say you left it all on the field and had nothing left to give. The desire to be the best you can be cannot be taught. You must acquire it. It is that desire to be the best you can be that will push you further than the average person could ever go.

8. Destroy All Doubt

The next action step is to destroy all doubt. There will be times when you just don't know what to do next and you have no idea how you are going to make it. It is in those times that you must have faith and belief in God, yourself, and the process. If you have just one percent doubt, you're out.

Doubt has no place in a successful person's psyche. If you have properly planned your steps and you are walking in divine order, then where does doubt fit in? Doubt is an enemy of success that must be met head on and destroyed. Doubt is simply fear repackaged. God has not given us the spirit of fear so whenever you feel doubt trying to creep in ask yourself three questions: 1) Have I properly prepared for this moment? 2) Am I following God's purpose for my life? 3) If I answered, "Yes" to one and two then, what am I afraid of?

Believe it or not, some people are afraid of being successful. They doubt that success is really for them. They eventually sabotage their life by listening to every excuse of the enemy as to why they are not good enough or why they cannot succeed like others. Doubt is a dangerous enemy that, when left alone, will not only destroy your purpose but it will spread among all those around you. Doubt is not your friend. When you feel it coming you must destroy it immediately.

9. Don't Waste Time

Have you ever felt like there just aren't enough hours in a day to get things done? Does it seem like your To-Do List gets longer each day? Is your middle name Procrastination? Perhaps your problem is not the lack of time but the lack of time management. Let me give you one piece of advice that will help you better manage your time. Throw away your To-Do List!

A To-Do List is one of the worst enemies to a successful person. To gain better time management, successful people go from a To-Do List to a Schedule. What good is a laundry list of things to do if you have no plan for when you need to start and complete each one? Most people make a To-Do List with the goal to complete it sometime today, but a schedule spells out what to do, when to do it and how long it should take to do it. Scheduling your time is much more effective than just going through each day doing things whenever you get to them.

Your To-Do List is your starting point; unfortunately, most people also make it their ending point. Your goal is to create a daily schedule for yourself that will ensure you take advantage of every minute. Once you list everything you hope to achieve (To-Do List), you must assign priority to each task. Starting with the highest priority, determine how long it will take you to complete that task and what time you will start. Put that task in your planner and continue through your list doing the same thing for each task. You have now created a schedule. Sticking to your schedule and handling the highest priority tasks first will improve your time management and help you minimize wasted time.

10. Don't Ever Quit

The final step in your game plan is don't ever quit. I know a few chapters ago I said it's OK to quit but understand the nuance here. It's OK to quit and recalibrate on the who, what, when, where, and/or how, but never quit on the why. Be patient along your journey and do not get discouraged when things do not go just as you planned. God has already promised your success but it's up to you to remain steadfast and unmovable along the way. No great feat has ever been accomplished without overcoming some type of struggle and the same is true for achieving success. Never quitting is what makes successful people so special.

It may be easy to pack your bags and count your losses when the road you're treading gets rough. But it is difficult to live the rest of your life as a quitter wondering what might have been. Right now, your storm may seem too treacherous to weather and it is hard to keep going but life will be much easier and more peaceful once you unfold your potential and are walking in your destiny. It takes a special individual to go against the grain of common logic and to never quit.

Each challenge in your life represents a fork in the road to success. It is at your crossroads where a life-altering decision must be made. Do I quit or do I go on? Do I live a comfortable life now and spend my twilight years uncomfortably or do I deal with the discomfort now and spend the rest of my life in comfort? Ninety-seven percent of people choose comfort now and end up paying for it down the line while only three percent choose to deal with the pain now to live a lifetime of comfort.

People around you are not going to understand why you keep trying different businesses, going after lofty dreams, or will not get a "real" job, but those same people, five to ten years from now, will not understand why you are living the lifestyle they could only dream of living. The only difference between the 97% and the 3% is that the 3% never quit on their dreams. Remember, success does not happen in a day, it happens daily.

GRADUATION DAY

Congratulations! You did it! If over the last fifty-two weeks you have committed to the lessons to become a better personal leader; then undoubtedly that will translate into you growing into a better leader of others. You cannot wait until a position opens before you go and acquire the necessary skills to fill that opening. You must commit your life to becoming that person before you actually become that person.

I really want to stress that leadership is not about a title. You can lead from anywhere in your life. If you practice these lessons, you will become a person of significant influence and that is all leadership really is anyway. If you currently lead other people, then I would encourage you to purchase a copy of this book for each of them so that they too can learn how to become better leaders. I cannot think of a better way to teach leadership to your organization than through this manual.

I would love to hear your feedback on this book so please send me a comment to ryan@ryancgreene.com. If you enjoyed the book and stand behind the product then I encourage you to make some noise to everyone you know and tell anyone that will listen about this book. Be sure to visit www.ryancgreene.com and join my email list to help spread the word. You can also gain access to more resources and training.

All my life I have been thrust into leadership roles. People have always come to me for answers and guidance. That being said, I still know that by no means do I have all the answers. I am constantly learning more and growing in my own leadership. I am a student of so many great leaders who have come before me. I want to thank all the leaders in my industry that I look to when I need answers.

In closing I would just like to remind you that "You do not need a title to be a leader; you need a purpose." Each of us has been given a purpose for which to lead and it's up to you to find yours. Though the road at times may be lonely, you can never allow yourself to settle for good enough. You were designed for greatness. You are an excellent leader. I wish you the best.
CLASS DISMISSED.

God Bless!

ABOUT YOUR PROFESSOR

As the visionary founder of GreeneHouse Media, Ryan C. Greene, "The Passionpreneur", has carved a niche for himself in the visual media and leadership development industries. Whether he's gracing the stage in front of thousands, captivating audiences over the airwaves, or sharing his wisdom through the pages of his 11 bestselling books, Ryan is the go-to authority for leaders, speakers, and authors seeking to master, magnify, and monetize their unique message through the power of visual media. His focus is on producing and directing premium-quality, impactful, and entertaining visual media platforms that empower leaders and brands to 10x their influence, impact, and income by effectively conveying their stories through media.

One of Ryan's most remarkable creations is the Born To Be Dope® Brand, a groundbreaking fusion of hip-hop and personal development that spotlights the stories and voices of our culture's most influential leaders and influencers. This dynamic brand encompasses visual mixtapes in the form of feature films, enriching audiobooks, lively conferences, a captivating TV show, a thought-provoking podcast, and a distinctive clothing line that celebrates the art of being unapologetically great at being yourself. Ryan's ingenious work has garnered recognition on major media platforms such as ABC, CBS, NBC, Fox, The Washington Post, and various other esteemed outlets.

With humble beginnings as a book publisher in 2005, Ryan's journey has led him to author 11 impactful books. In addition to his impressive literary contributions, he has founded Indie Author PRO, a cutting-edge author marketing strategy company. This venture is dedicated to helping independent authors seamlessly publish, promote, and profit like seasoned professionals. Ryan's expertise now extends to bringing authors' books and wisdom to life on screen through his renowned Beyond The Book Visual Storytellers Series.

273

Away from the spotlight, Ryan resides in Maryland with his beloved wife, Tyneka, and is the proud father of two accomplished adult children, Jordan and Jayden. His commitment to empowering others to share their stories and make a positive impact continues to be the driving force behind his work, ensuring that he remains a prominent figure in the world of visual media and personal development.

For more information or to book Ryan C. Greene to speak for your organization or to present at your next event, please visit www.RyanCGreene.com or email Ryan@RyanCGreene.com

Watch **Ryan C. Greene's BORN TO BE DOPE**! on the
GHM TV app, Apple TV, Roku TV, Fire TV, YouTube or
listen to the audio podcast.

Available on all streaming platforms.

Follow @iamborntobedope on Instagram.

Get your FREE Setting S.T.U.P.I.D. Goals
audio training now at
www.settingstupidgoals.com